The Secret of Teams

The Secret of Teams

WHAT GREAT TEAMS KNOW AND DO

Mark Miller

BK

Berrett–Koehler Publishers, Inc.
San Francisco
a BK Business book

Copyright 2011 © by Mark Miller

Berrett-Koehler Publishers, Inc.
235 Montgomery Street, Suite 650
San Francisco, CA 94104-2916
Tel: (415) 288-0260   Fax: (415) 362-2512   www.bkconnection.com

Ordering Information
Quantity sales. Special discounts are available on quantity purchases by corporations, associations, and others. For details, contact the "Special Sales Department" at the Berrett-Koehler address above.
Individual sales. Berrett-Koehler publications are available through most bookstores. They can also be ordered directly from Berrett-Koehler: Tel: (800) 929-2929; Fax: (802) 864-7626; www.bkconnection.com
Orders for college textbook/course adoption use. Please contact Berrett-Koehler: Tel: (800) 929-2929; Fax: (802) 864-7626.
Orders by U.S. trade bookstores and wholesalers. Please contact Ingram Publisher Services, Tel: (800) 509-4887; Fax: (800) 838-1149; E-mail: customer .service@ingrampublisherservices.com; or visit www.ingrampublisherservices.com/ Ordering for details about electronic ordering.

Berrett-Koehler and the BK logo are registered trademarks of Berrett-Koehler Publishers, Inc.

Printed in the United States of America

Berrett-Koehler books are printed on long-lasting acid-free paper. When it is available, we choose paper that has been manufactured by environmentally responsible processes. These may include using trees grown in sustainable forests, incorporating recycled paper, minimizing chlorine in bleaching, or recycling the energy produced at the paper mill.

Production Management: Michael Bass Associates
Cover Design: Irene Morris

Library of Congress Cataloging-in-Publication Data
Miller, Mark, 1959-
    The secret of teams : what great teams know and do / Mark Miller.
        p. cm.
    ISBN 978-1-60994-093-5 (hardcover : alk. paper)
    1. Teams in the workplace. I. Title.
HD66.M5446 2011
658.4'022—dc23   2011023839

First Edition
16 15 14 • 10 9 8 7 6 5 4

I dedicate this project to my family:
Thank you for your love,
encouragement, and prayers!

Contents

Foreword

By Ken Blanchard

When it comes to writing a book about teams, I can think of few people more qualified than my friend, Mark Miller, Vice President of Training and Development for Chick-fil-A. Mark and I have known each other for more than a decade. Over the years, we've worked together on several projects in the marketplace and in the not-for-profit world. Soon after we met, he and I teamed up to write *The Secret: What Great Leaders Know and Do*, which has become an international best-seller.

Fortunately for readers, Mark has been a student and a practitioner of teams for the last twenty years. I'm glad he's committed to sharing what he's learned on that journey. An accomplished communicator, he brings clarity to the often complex subject of building winning teams. In *The Secret of Teams*, he shares elemental truths about teams that, if employed, can transform not only your team but every aspect of your business. In the pages that follow, he'll show you how to create teams that can sustain unprecedented levels of performance.

So let this book inspire you and your team to give your management, shareholders, vendors, partners, and customers more than they expect. Whether you're part of a huge corporation, a not-for-profit organization, or a small company with just a few employees, apply the principles and practices in *The Secret of Teams* to make your workplace come alive!

— Ken Blanchard,
Coauthor of *The One Minute Manager*® and
Leading at a Higher Level

Introduction
An Amazing Journey

Teams are certainly not a new idea. Most of us have had some experience participating on a team. It may have been a sports team, a debate team, a team organized to solve a problem, as part of a nonprofit organization or maybe a team at work. As a result of our individual experiences, we will each read the pages that follow with a point of view informed by our past. However, I want to encourage you to put those experiences behind you because most of us have had team experiences that were far from ideal—most of us have never been part of a true high-performance team.

If you can approach the idea of teams with fresh eyes, you could be on the verge of a tremendous breakthrough. A breakthrough in performance, a breakthrough in the development of people, a breakthrough in your own leadership capacity, and perhaps most importantly, you could experience a breakthrough in your quality of life. I realize that's a lot to promise from the simple story that follows. However, this promise is not based on the power of the story; rather, it is based on the power of the ideas represented here and my belief in the tremendous untapped potential of your team.

Getting people to work together to achieve exceptional, sustained results is more difficult to deliver than it is to discuss. Pursuing high-performance teams as a strategy for improved performance is messy and extremely challenging. But the size of the challenge is just one reason why the idea itself represents such an inviting approach for creating competitive advantage.

This book contains simple ideas that can revolutionize your team and its performance, but none of them will be possible without your leadership. At the end of this book, you'll have a decision to make: *What will you do next?*

In an attempt to help you answer that question, I've included some suggested action items and a High-Performance Team Assessment. I hope you'll find these tools helpful as you chart your course.

Get ready to multiply your leadership, leverage the talent of your people, and generate remarkable results . . . get ready for an amazing journey!

—Mark Miller

Study the Best

Debbie was discouraged. Her new team was proving to be more of a challenge than she had bargained for. Up to this point in her career, she had enjoyed success after success. Most noteworthy, she had led her previous dysfunctional team "from worst to first." This feat had not gone unnoticed by management. In fact, Jeff, the CEO, had given Debbie her recent promotion in part due to her success and in part because he saw tremendous potential in her.

However, in her new role, nothing seemed to be going her way. With her former team, she had looked forward to every new day, but now she went to work only to be confronted by a team with real issues. Not only that, Debbie was feeling the stress and strain of trying to do more and more, often with less resources. Beyond her team issues, she was faced with a growing mountain of e-mail; there seemed to be more meetings than ever; and if there was any time left, she still had customers to serve. She was tired. The pace of her life was out of control, and she wasn't sure what to do about it.

Besides her immediate issues, she had heard rumors that scores of other leaders and their teams across the company were also struggling. Evidence of this could be seen as the customer base was eroding and the stock price was sliding.

Debbie knew that in her role, she was supposed to help the organization resolve these issues; but in her heart she knew that before she could help others, she would need to start with her leadership, her team, and her own life.

She decided to take the matter up with Jeff. Not only had he served as her mentor several years before, but he had continued to provide valuable counsel over the years. Thankfully, he always seemed to have the time—or make the time—to see her when it really mattered.

"I just don't know what to do," she admitted to him candidly.

"I understand, Debbie. You want things to work. You want your team to excel. That's one of the traits we value about you."

She beamed, despite the circumstances that had brought her to Jeff's office.

"So how can I help?" Jeff asked.

"Well, you could tell me what you've done to create such an effective team. How do you achieve such alignment and outstanding performance from your executive team?"

Jeff thought carefully before responding. "I wish I had a magic formula to give you, but I don't." He paused. "Remember years ago when you asked me about the secret of great leaders?"

"I do. As it turned out, it was the best question I think I've ever asked." Debbie was almost overwhelmed as she thought about how that single question, and Jeff's response, changed her life and her leadership style forever.

"Today, I'm turning the tables," Jeff said. "I need you to find the secret of great teams."

"Where should I start?" Debbie asked.

"Study the best."

"What do you mean by that?" she asked.

"Find teams that are doing it right. They don't have to be teams in our company. You can go outside. Look any-where you want. The truth is, we *need* answers."

There was a tone in Jeff's voice that Debbie had never heard before. She decided to probe a little further.

"Thanks for the advice, Jeff. Based on what you're saying, combined with the rumors I've heard, it sounds like this assignment is much bigger than the issues I'm dealing with when it comes to my team." There was clearly a question in her tone.

Jeff hesitated for just a second before he responded. "I thought you'd probably heard the buzz. Our company is in trouble. Thanks to increased competition, increased costs, and some other issues we're trying to uncover, we're struggling. We're even worried about a hostile takeover bid. The answers that you discover in your quest to help your team excel may help other teams within our organization. Are you willing to take on that challenge?"

"I am!" Debbie replied confidently. "And I promise I won't let you down!"

. . .

Debbie took Jeff's challenge back to her office and began to prepare for her team meeting. This sounded like the most important thing she had worked on during her career. In many ways, it was similar to the challenges that she had faced as a young leader, but this time they were multiplied a thousandfold. She now realized that it wasn't just her team struggling; it was the entire organization.

She understood the assignment, but she wanted to get a better grasp of the underlying problem before she launched her work.

How did we get in this situation? she wondered.

To find the answer, she began to make a list. Unfortunately, the ideas flowed all too easily. She wrote the following:

How did we get in the state of affairs we're in today?

- *More competition than ever.*
- *Increasing complexity in the business—it's just harder than it used to be.*

- *More demanding customers—they have higher expectations than ever!*
- *Our leaders are struggling to get it all done—they have reached their capacity.*

Debbie decided quickly that her next step would be to involve her team in helping her "study the best." She knew that would not be easy. Since she had left the Operations Group and become the head of Leadership Development, she had to work with what remained of a team that had never been very effective. Their next meeting was in two days, and Jeff's new assignment would be the focus of the meeting.

. . .

By 9:00, everyone had arrived for their weekly meeting, and Debbie said, "Good morning!" in her usual warm and personable style. "It's really good to see all of you again. Let's take a few minutes to reconnect. What's going on in your life?"

One by one, members of the team shared an update. There seemed to be some reluctance at first, but as people began to open up a little, it was quickly apparent that what they wanted to talk about were things outside of work.

Tom bragged about his new grandbaby, with pictures, of course. Javier said that his mother was coming from his home country to visit—she'd be with him for a month. He told the team that he hadn't seen her in two years.

Jo shared an update on her mom. The previous weekend, the family had placed her in hospice care—her illness was too severe for additional treatment. The group saw the sadness in Jo's eyes. Although none of them had personally experienced what she was going through, they were trying to understand her pain.

After Jo finished, the team was quiet. Debbie was sensitive to the moment. "We all have a lot to be thankful for, and we all have a lot we need help with. I'm glad we have one another for the journey."

There was a long silence. Everyone now had shared an update except Steve. Debbie looked at him to see if he wanted to say anything; he didn't. Debbie decided to move the meeting forward. "I know you received the agenda for today's meeting, but I'm going to make a change. As you're all aware, the business has really been struggling. I met with Jeff on Friday, and he's given us an assignment. He's asked us to help take our teams across the organization to the next level."

"What exactly does that mean?" asked Javier, in a respectful tone.

"Well," Debbie said, "what do you guys think?"

"Okay, wait a minute," Jo jumped into the conversation. "You met with Jeff? The fact that you're asking for our input means he didn't tell you, right?"

"Well, he told me part of the answer . . . ."

Steve interrupted her in a tone that reflected his impatience with the conversation. "What *exactly* is the problem we're actually trying to solve?"

Debbie ignored Steve's sarcastic tone and thanked him for his question. Based on his question, she decided to take an opportunity to tell the team about some of the issues facing the business. She spoke briefly about complexity, competition, growing customer expectations, and leadership capacity constraints. Then she said, "So, Jeff believes that our teams are the best way for us to turn around our performance. Here's something to think about: where do you think our teams are on a scale of 1 to 10?"

Bob joined the conversation. "That's not a fair question."

"Why not?" Debbie pushed for a response.

"We have hundreds of teams around the world. They are all over the board. Some are a 10 and others are a 1," Bob said.

Javier said, "Some aren't even a 1 yet." They had talked about the state of teams before. It was widely known that although every business unit *said* they were organized in a team structure, in truth, many were not teams at all.

"Okay, exactly what is the assignment?" Then Jo attempted to answer her own question. "Are we supposed to help each team in the organization go to the next level— whatever that may be for them?"

Although every business unit said *they were organized in a team structure, in truth, many were not teams at all.*

"Yes, that's part of it," Debbie responded.

"There's more?" Bob asked.

"Yes. Jeff challenged us to 'study the best.'"

"And . . . ." Jo paused.

Debbie finished her sentence: "We get to figure that out. We get to decide who we'll learn from on this topic."

"Don't we already know the answer?" Javier said.

"Yeah," Bob joined in. "Debbie, you're a rock star around here. When you were in Operations, you took your team from worst to first. You had an amazing team back then."

"And what are we, chopped liver?" Sally smiled.

"Chop, chop," Steve muttered under his breath. Everyone ignored him.

"Jeff believes we're the right team to take on this task, even though I told him that we've got a lot of room for improvement ourselves," Debbie said. "He still insists that we can help the entire organization take our teams to the next level. And who knows? Maybe we'll grow in the process."

"So why can't we just tell Jeff and the rest of the organization what you did in Operations?" Javier rephrased his question.

"Prophets are not accepted in their own land," Sally said.

"Is that in the Bible?" Jo whispered to Tom.

"I don't know, but if it's not, it should be." Tom grinned.

"You know what I mean," Debbie continued. "We want to enhance the credibility of our message by validating it in other situations—inside our company and in other organizations."

"So in summary . . . ." Jo was always good at helping the group with closure. She went to the flip chart and wrote:

Our business challenges
    Complexity, competition, customer expectations, and leadership capacity

Our assignment
    Help our leaders take their teams to the next level

Our first step
    Study the best

"Great summary," Debbie said.

"So who do we study?" Tom was curious.

"Let's talk about that." Debbie wanted the team's input on this decision. She asked the group, "where do we see examples of Great Teams?"

This started a rather awkward brainstorming session and discussion. There were plenty of ideas. However, Debbie had to constantly challenge the group to suspend judgment. After a lengthy session, the team created a list of more than forty different organizations or groups in which the presence of a strong team was obvious. After an hour of debate, the group had shortened their list to ten options. They knew that was still too many, but it represented progress. Here's what they had so far:

Where do we see examples of great teams?

Emergency Room Staff	Football Team
Firefighters	Special Forces in the Military
Orchestra	Auto Racing Team
Cycling Team	A Local Restaurant Company
A Large Church	Broadway Play Company

With that list made, the team had a brief discussion about the pros and cons of each of the options.

In the end, they decided to eliminate the football and cycling teams. Although they agreed they could certainly learn from both of these, they felt that traditional team sports as the predominant illustration for teamwork had been overused. They would look for their best practices in other fields.

"Let's do this as a next step," Debbie suggested. "What if we each do a little research on our own? Let's think about who we may know who could help us. We'll bring our findings to our next meeting. Then we can chase the hot leads."

The team was still skeptical about Jeff's assignment. However, Debbie could sense the seed of excitement in their conversation. This project was going to help the company and their leaders; it would expand their own world as they looked outside their company for best practices; she was hopeful that it would help her team go to the next level; and it would probably be fun, too!

Truth Is Truth

As the team left the room, Debbie had already decided she wanted to get a meeting on Jeff's calendar to get input on their list. He was really well connected, and she was confident he could make some introductions. To make their time more productive, she decided to send him an e-mail in advance.

Jeff,

Our team met today. We did some brainstorming, re: your encouragement to **study the best**. We've not yet finalized our choices. We're looking for input and connections. I'm going to get a short meeting on the calendar for us to talk about our next steps. To make that time more productive, here's what we're considering:

- Emergency Room Staff
- Firefighters
- Auto Racing Team
- A Local Restaurant Company
- Special Forces in the Military
- Orchestra
- A Large Church
- Broadway Play Company

I look forward to your input. We'll talk soon!

Deb

As she hit the Send key, she couldn't help but think about the options. She felt her team could learn a lot from all of these organizations. Any of them could help their teams move to the next level. She had so many questions. What would they learn? Would they hear the same things from each of these very different teams? How would the lessons learned match her experience? She sensed it was going to be an amazing journey.

Debbie was excited to find that Jeff was available for a meeting in just a few days. On the day of the meeting she went to his office, which had been her practice now for many years. There was something encouraging about the space. The unassuming décor and his welcoming spirit made it very inviting, the kind of place where collaboration and innovation were common occurrences.

"Good to see you again." Jeff greeted Debbie at the door with a warm smile and a firm handshake.

"Yes, it's good to see you again, too." Debbie smiled. "I know we just met last week, but I wanted to spend a few minutes to see what you think about the direction we're taking on this project."

"Thanks for checking in. I think you're on the right track. Anything else?"

Debbie knew this was Jeff's attempt at humor. She decided to play along.

"No, that's all. Thanks." She got up to leave.

"Wait," Jeff said.

"There's more?" Debbie exclaimed in an exaggerated tone—but with a smile.

"Yes. Don't forget *your* experience with this topic."

"What do you mean by that?"

"I still stand by the idea of 'study the best.' However, don't think about that exclusively as an 'outside-the-organization' idea. We need to study our best, as well. We can't do that without learning from your success with your team in Operations. You brought a team from worst to first, and contrary to what you currently believe, you appear to be making great strides with your current team. I think you know a lot about building outstanding teams."

"Thanks, Jeff. I feel very fortunate to have been part of a great team in the past. And . . . I pray that my current team can go to the next level as well. However, I don't want to bias the process by injecting my past experience."

"I have a thought and a suggestion."

"Please," Debbie said, notepad in hand.

"Don't undervalue your experience. You have done

The keys to building great teams are universal.

---

what we're trying to help others do. I admire your restraint regarding 'the answer.' I think we agree the answer may look different for different teams.

"Here's my suggestion: Capture your thoughts on how to build a great team—based on what you learned while you were in Operations. You don't even have to share them with anyone. The visits that you and your team are about to make will be even more interesting for you if you are able to compare what you find with your own experience. I'm actually quite confident that what you're going to find are the same principles manifested in many different ways. Truth is truth. I believe the keys to building great teams are universal."

"We'll find out. Thanks, Jeff."

This time as Debbie headed to the door, Jeff added one more thing. "If you decide to explore the Special Forces, I know someone who would help. I'll send you an e-mail with his contact info and a brief bio."

"Thanks! That would be very helpful."

Debbie left feeling on track. She liked Jeff's idea of capturing the key lessons from her past experiences. She also agreed with him that she shouldn't share her answers with the team before they made their visits. She wanted to see what principles and practices they would discover without her input. She'd record her thoughts regarding what she believed to be true about creating a great team and put it in a sealed envelope. Then, she'd give it to one of her teammates to be opened when the team finished their work.

When Debbie returned to her workspace, she had already received an e-mail from Jeff. In typical form, Jeff had not only helped, but he had helped in a major way. She read the e-mail and was excited about the possibilities.

Deb,

Here's the name of someone who might be helpful:

Brigadier General Roger Grant (retired)

Special Forces Commander

35 years of distinguished service; served in Vietnam, Desert Storm, Iraq, Pakistan, Afghanistan, and probably a lot of other places he can't tell you about. Roger and I have become friends. We serve on the board of a nonprofit together. If you decide you want to arrange a visit, I'll be happy to make the introduction.

Let me know how I can serve you. Thanks for your leadership on this project!

Jeff

Debbie thought, *Wow!* She would want the team to weigh in on this, but it was certainly an incredible lead.

At the next team meeting, they began as usual with a time of catching up. There was again a mix of business and personal information. Jo reported that her mother's health was declining rapidly.

"We're sorry to hear that," Tom offered. "Anything we can do to help?"

"Well . . . I'm not sure right now, but thanks for asking."

Javier added, "You don't need to do this all by yourself. Let us know what we can do."

"I will. I'll keep you posted. Right now, it's mostly waiting."

Debbie was glad the team was trying to help Jo. This was a huge sign of progress. This attitude of caring about people as people, not just coworkers, was one of the things she always tried to nurture in the team—a willingness, even an eagerness, to help one another.

Debbie looked at their agenda and said, "We've got one big topic today. Where will we go to study the best? Has anyone had any insights or found any good leads?"

The group began to share one by one what their independent research had revealed. Debbie shared the contact that Jeff had provided.

The team quickly decided not to pursue several of the remaining ideas. The list was getting shorter and more focused as the team continued to debate each of the finalists.

"I've got a great contact with the racing team. It's a NASCAR hookup," said Sally. "My husband's company is one of the sponsors of a car. He thinks we can get access to the cars, the drivers, and the owners."

"That sounds easy," Javier said. "Let's do that one."

The group agreed.

"Okay. Somebody help me with the restaurant company. That feels too different from us. Besides, what could we possibly learn from them?" Jo didn't conceal her concern regarding this option.

"Good question," Debbie said. "Any responses?"

Tom said, "I have to confess, I felt the same way as Jo two weeks ago. However, I did some research, and I've changed my mind."

"Why?" Jo asked.

"Three reasons: These guys are good. They've won numerous national awards for food and service. They execute with excellence—consistently. They're in a high-turnover industry, just like we are. Yet, they've figured out how to do this in thousands of locations all over the world. We have to figure that out, too. We have operations in thirty-five states and fourteen countries. We're not as big as they are, but they've figured out how to make teams work at a high level in a decentralized model."

"That's a compelling argument, I think," Jo said. "I'm in." Everyone else agreed.

"So that leaves the emergency room. What do we want to do with that one?" Javier asked.

"I don't like blood," said Steve.

"Me neither," said Jo. "Besides, I've spent way too much time in hospitals in the last three years."

Debbie said, "Here's my proposal: Let's go with the Special Forces, the NASCAR team, and the restaurant. If we need more information after that, we can always revisit our list. And if we choose the emergency room . . . ."

Steve interrupted, "I'll let someone have my seat on that trip."

"Me, too," Jo added.

Debbie closed the conversation. "That sounds like a plan. Let's get started."

The Three Pillars

The team was excited about its first visit. Everyone knew the reputation of the Special Forces as an elite unit of dedicated professional service members who get results. As Debbie prepared for the visit, she couldn't help but wonder if the general would share the same principles that she believed were essential to creating high performance in a team.

The team had decided to split the assignments, and they agreed to let Jo stay home with her mom. On this trip, Debbie would be joined by Tom and Javier.

As they approached the general's home, Debbie wasn't sure what to expect. However, she did have in her mind what she thought the general would look like—a classic Army general, the type you'd see in the movies. Her stereotype was about to be challenged.

When Debbie and her team arrived at the address they had been given, they were greeted by a man that she assumed was the general, but he didn't look at all like what she had imagined. She knew he was retired, but she hadn't expected him to be so old. He was short, too; for some reason, she had thought he would be taller.

"Hello, General Grant," she said with a bit of a question in her voice. "My name is Debbie."

He stopped her, "Dear, please call me Roger. I was a general once, but I'll always be Roger." He smiled.

Debbie had expected the tone of a drill sergeant barking orders, not the warmth she encountered. He spoke softly. "Please, come in."

"Yes, sir. Thank you. This is Tom and Javier. We really appreciate you sharing your time and your experience with us."

"It's my pleasure. I love to serve whenever I can," he added.

Debbie thought, *That makes sense. He and Jeff are friends. Jeff believes that the best leaders serve. And here we are meeting the general, and in the first two minutes, he's talking about serving. I don't think that's a coincidence. One of them has clearly influenced the other.*

Roger continued, "How's Jeff?"

"He's doing really well. Our business is under some intense pressure right now, but I'm confident in his leadership," Debbie said.

"I share your confidence. Nothing clarifies your thinking like an imminent threat. My money is on Jeff and your team meeting all the challenges you face. May I offer you something to drink?"

The group declined his offer.

"That's fine. I'm going to have tea. Have a seat here in the living room, and I'll get the tea and some extra cups. You may change your mind."

When Roger returned from the kitchen, he sat down and immediately asked, "Specifically, how may I help you?"

"We think we can best meet the challenges we face in our organization by helping our leaders build stronger teams," Tom said.

"I agree completely," Roger said.

"So, we want to talk to you about what makes the Special Forces units such strong teams," Javier said.

"How much time do you have?" Roger chuckled. "That's how I invested most of my time as a leader for over thirty years."

"Well, it sounds like we've come to see the right person," Debbie observed. "Can you share some of what you've learned from your experience?"

"Certainly!" Roger seemed energized by the opportunity.

As he began to talk, it was clear that he had given this topic a lot of thought.

"I have discovered that there are three pillars that support the success of a team," he began. "The first you can call **selection**.

"It matters who is on the team. We were very diligent in our selection process. We had very high standards that were clearly articulated and rigorously enforced. We didn't accept just anyone on our team. We wanted people who had the attitude and the aptitude for the job. This is intended to be an elite group. I don't mean elite as in arrogant. I do mean that it was and still is a select group. Is that clear?"

Tom asked, "What happened when you got the wrong person on the team?"

"When we made a mistake in the selection process, we would move quickly to take corrective action."

"How did you handle that?" Javier wasn't sure he really wanted to know what corrective action meant in the military, but he asked anyway.

Roger responded, "Depending on the issue, reassignment or discharge were our options."

The group continued to talk about selection for almost an hour. They probed the criteria to be part of Special Forces, the selection process, and more. Several of Roger's thoughts were accompanied by very interesting stories.

Then, without much of a transition, Roger said, "The second pillar is **training**.

"We were a training machine. A team can't really be a team if its members don't know what they're doing. And we found that repetition was our friend. Continuous training helped keep the team sharp."

Debbie had a question: "Roger, what kind of training?"

Roger responded, "All types. Job- and role-specific, hard and soft skills, combat and survival, the skills of leadership and management, team skills, problem solving, decision making . . . and the list goes on and on."

"I don't think about many of those things when I think about Special Forces," admitted Javier.

"Nor should you," said Roger. "However, those things are the reason you have such a high opinion of the Special Forces. You're not supposed to see the process, just the out-

---

A team can't really be a team if its members don't know what they're doing.

---

come. Training is a key driver for superior performance that is replicable over time—and in ever-changing situations. Training is the mother of consistency. Without extreme levels of training, you can't predict the outcome with any level of certainty. And when the Special Forces are involved, we want to do *everything* we can to bring about a positive outcome. Most often, lives are at stake."

Roger stopped and sipped his tea. "Questions?"

"Was there resistance to so much training?" Javier asked.

"Certainly, but it was one of the nonnegotiables. Our soldiers clearly understood why we were training. Staying alive is usually sufficient motivation. However, there's nothing that really makes you want to jump out of a helicopter into the North Sea in a training exercise. It's *really* cold." Roger grinned in such a way that the three visitors all had the same thought: *He probably loved it!*

"Any other questions about training?" Roger asked.

The team had a few other questions about the specific team-related skills he taught his soldiers. Once again, he was gracious and answered every question.

Javier, wanting to be sure they had ample time for the next topic, said, "Roger, you mentioned a third pillar?"

"Yes, I call it **esprit de corps**."

"Is that Latin?" Tom asked.

"It's French."

"What exactly does it mean?" Debbie only had a vague idea.

Roger said, "It means 'group spirit.' Or to put it another way, 'a strong sense of enthusiasm and dedication that unites a group.'"

"Tell us why that's the third pillar," Javier said.

"That's what makes all the difference. It's really the 'secret sauce.' Many teams that are good never become great because of this missing ingredient. Some leaders see it as too soft or too vague or too elusive. It may be all three, but it is *extremely* powerful. When it exists, men and women will sacrifice their lives for their comrades. They'll endure extreme hardship for the sake of others on the team. They'll work harder and longer because of this element. This is not the head stuff that you can drill in through training. This is the heart stuff. It's where great achievement ultimately comes from. That's why I said earlier that training was *one* of the drivers of superior performance. Training is critical, but it's for the head. Esprit de corps is about the heart. Particularly when things get really hard, it becomes an even bigger part of achieving high performance."

Debbie felt that very few people had seen this level of commitment before. "How do you create it?"

"It takes some time," Roger said, "and you have to be deliberate. However, don't miss the point."

"And that is . . . ." Tom was quite sure he'd already missed it.

"The point is, your team will *never* perform at the highest possible level if the members of the team don't exhibit genuine care and concern for one another. The best leaders create an environment where this is the norm. And once it is achieved, they work diligently to maintain that culture.

"In summary, to create extraordinary team performance, the leader must focus on the three pillars of **selection**, **training**, and **esprit de corps**. Any questions?"

"I've got a question that feels related to me," Javier said. "With all this talk about teams, how does that impact decision making?"

Your team will never *perform at the highest possible level if the members of the team don't exhibit genuine care and concern for one another.*

"There's a misconception about the military in general. It revolves around *command and control*. While there is always a place for this type of decision making—and perhaps more often in the military—it is not the path to high performance over the long haul. I knew I had a critical role to play in the success of the Special Forces, and every leader in our organization knew that, too. However, we had to create teams that could work without us—small teams that could make decisions in a hurry, often with limited information, and most likely, the difficulty was compounded by the urgency of the situation.

"In a true command-and-control scenario, the leader would make *all* the decisions. That's certainly not feasible, nor would it be desirable. The more decisions a leader makes, the further he or she is from leading a high-performing team. Leaders who make too many command decisions don't get more responsibility. Over time, they get less. Make too many command decisions, and you'll doom yourself and your team to mediocrity."

"Wow! I never thought about it like that," Javier admitted.

"Anything else you'd like to talk about?" Roger asked.

Debbie and the team asked a few follow-up questions and then thanked Roger for his time.

"It's been my pleasure," he said warmly. "I don't get to talk about these things much anymore. Thanks for coming. Please tell Jeff I said hello!"

"I will!" Debbie replied.

Winning Is Hard Work

Following the successful visit with the general, Debbie was more excited than ever. The next visit would take the team to North Carolina—the epicenter for America's largest spectator sport, NASCAR. Because they selected an "off-week" to visit the track, Debbie and her group would have access to key members of the top racing team of the last decade. The meeting was scheduled to take place early on a Tuesday morning. Bob and Sally would accompany Debbie on this visit, since it was Sally's husband who had the connection with NASCAR.

They got to the track early. As they approached, they were overwhelmed by the mammoth size of the facility. On race day, up to 140,000 fans would descend on the property. It was truly a spectacular venue for a death-defying, high-speed, adrenaline-filled event.

They made their way through security and went into a tunnel. When they came out, they realized they had just gone under the track. They were now in the infield pit area, surrounded by tens of thousands of empty seats.

As they stood looking around, awestruck at the scope of it all, the spell was broken when someone called out, "Hey, there! What can I do for you?"

Bob introduced himself and the team and gave a brief explanation for their visit. He then told the man they were there to see the Mullins Team.

"Follow me. I'll be glad to take you to their office."

When they arrived, they realized this wasn't going to be a typical office visit. The office was actually in a transporter truck, parked on the infield among many other similar trucks. For Bob, this was a dream come true; he'd been a NASCAR fan for years.

The truck itself was like a workshop, but with amenities. There was a kitchen, or "galley," workbench area with parts storage bins, and even storage areas for extra engines. A ramp allowed for two race cars to be transported on the upper level of the truck, above the busy work areas below.

As they stood there taking it all in, they were approached by a big man in his late fifties with a haircut like a Marine. Debbie thought to herself, *This is what I thought the general would look like.*

"Hi, I'm Sam Perkins, the head of Team Mullins," he said with a big smile.

"It's a pleasure to meet you. I'm Debbie; this is Sally and Bob."

Bob started the conversation. "Thanks for allowing us to visit. This is cool! I've never seen a truck decked out like this—you've got nicer furniture here than in my house." Sam laughed.

"And that flat-screen TV is the biggest I've ever seen," Sally added.

"Yes, it all helps create our home away from home. We spend a lot of time here," Sam said. "So what can I do for you today?"

"We're studying the best teams we can find, and you guys are at the top of your field," Debbie said.

"Thanks. We feel fortunate to be a winning team. Why do you want to study successful teams?"

"Well, the short answer is that we believe it will help our performance. The competition is heating up, the business is getting more complex, and our customers are continuing to expect more and more from us."

"We can relate to all of that. You just described the world we live in. One difference for us is that in addition to the paying customer who buys tickets to the events, we also have corporate sponsors. As you know, Sally's husband's company is one of them. They're great. However, they do expect us to win—and win often."

Debbie added, "There's one more factor in our current reality: our leaders are really tapped out. We're not sure how much more they can do. We believe that a team, functioning at a high level, will provide additional leadership capacity for them—not to mention physical, mental, and emotional capacity."

"Well, I'm happy to help in any way I can." Sam's relaxed manner made Debbie and her colleagues feel welcome.

"How do you do it? How do you get your team to perform at such a high level?"

"Let's talk about our pit crew. That's probably the best way to illustrate how we work together. We have numerous teams in our organization, but I think the pit crew is a great example of the power of teamwork.

"To get the six guys who work 'over the wall' to function at a consistently high level, there are at least three things that I think are critical."

Debbie's mind went immediately to the three things the general had shared. She wondered how Sam's thoughts would compare to those from the general—as well as with her own ideas.

"Please continue."

"First, there's the question of **fit**. Does the team member fit?"

Sally asked, "Do you mean fit in?"

"Yes, fitting in matters a lot, but there's more. Can they learn and grow? Are they coachable? What's their attitude—their outlook on life? It's more about who they are as people. Are they our kind of people?"

"When we talk about fit, we consider Character, Competency, and Chemistry," Debbie offered.

Sam said, "I like that. But it's those three and still more. Are they what we need? If a person is a great engine guy and we don't need an engine guy, he doesn't fit. He may be competent, but he still doesn't *fit* our need. He doesn't fill our gap."

"How can you tell if a person fits?" Bob asked.

"It's a process. We network extensively. We're always looking for people who fit. We conduct detailed interviews. We check references. We often start people in an entry-level role outside the pit crew and watch them. And then, we usually promote from within."

"Sounds like a lot of rigor for—." Debbie stopped in midsentence.

Sam said, "I know what you were going to say. It sounds like a lot of rigor for a car racing team. We prefer to think of it as diligence. As far as us just being a car racing team, that's correct. However, we have an organization of over a hundred people and a multimillion-dollar budget. We've won more than thirty races in the last decade, and our driver's life is on the line every time he gets in the car. We take our work very seriously. Besides, winning is hard work—diligence is required."

"I'm sorry, Sam. I really didn't mean it that way. I'm just impressed at your attention to details, particularly in the people arena. I'm fearful that many of our leaders may not take this part of their role seriously enough."

"It does all begin with people, but there's more to winning than the right people. The second thing that matters to us is **practice**," Sam said. "Practice is how we build skills, speed, and consistency."

"Please tell us how that works for you guys," Bob asked.

"We race thirty-six times a year, but we practice for hours virtually every week," Sam said.

"Tell us more about what practice means." Sally wasn't sure how the team would practice.

"The pit crew practices changing the tires and fueling the car. The driver obviously practices driving."

"Can you give us more background on the pit crew?" Debbie was trying to focus the conversation.

Practice is how we build skills, speed, and consistency.

"There are six primary roles on the crew. They fly into action every time the car rolls into the pit, because they only have thirteen or fourteen seconds to change the tires, fuel the car, and get it back on the track. Of course, each member has a specific assignment. We practice individually and as a team. And we do it over and over and over again. And, we're getting better."

"How do you know you're getting better?" Sally asked.

"The data."

"What data?" Bob asked.

"We measure everything," Sam said.

"Give us an example."

"When it comes to the pit crew, we measure every practice, every tire change, every refuel, and every pit stop."

"What are the advantages of measuring so much stuff?" Bob asked.

"A few things come to mind: Measurement tells us where we need to improve; it lets us know if our improvement efforts are working or not; it helps us stay focused; it brings out the best in us as a team; it presents a tangible challenge. This fuels continued improvement. We're always striving to beat our best—to shave off just one more second that the car is in the pit. And, maybe most importantly, it lets us know when to celebrate. I can't imagine being an effective leader without measurement."

"I had no idea measurement was so critical to your success," Debbie said.

I can't imagine being an effective leader without measurement.

"Measurement is a tool, just like a hammer or a wrench. It's a tool that helps us refine our skills. If we've got great people but they don't have the skills, we're no better off than if we had the wrong people. If we're going to win, we have to be both fast and consistent."

"What about cross-training?" Sally asked.

"We do some of that, but certain people are really best suited for a specific role. For example, see that young guy over there? His name is Chad. He's one of the youngest guys you'll see working on a crew. He was in our shop, and we noticed that he had amazing hand-eye coordination. So we asked him to try a few things with the car. He was really good. With practice, he's become outstanding! He can change a tire as fast as any seasoned veteran." Sam's excitement about Chad's accomplishments was obvious.

Debbie said, "I have a question. How did you discover that Chad had good hand-eye coordination?"

"We saw him juggling," Sam said.

"Juggling? You've got to be kidding," Bob laughed as he said it.

"Yep. He can really juggle—all kinds of things. It's quite a show."

"And you made the connection between juggling and working on the crew?"

Debbie was actually amazed. "Can you help us connect the dots?"

"That's one thing about our team I mentioned earlier. We're always looking for talented people. And we promote from within. Chad was already one of us. He was on the shop crew. As leaders, we have people with talent all around us—sometimes we just have to find them."

Sally candidly admitted, "I'm afraid that sometimes we get too busy to see the talent that's already on a team. I know it must feel great to give Chad a chance to move up."

"Yes, it *does* feel good. And who knows? He may ultimately drive for us."

"Really?" Debbie couldn't quite hide her surprise.

"Yes, ma'am. He wants to, and hand-eye coordination is a *big* deal for a driver—along with judgment, courage, patience, and maturity. Time will tell," Sam said.

"Last question about Chad." Bob couldn't resist, and again, the answer may have been obvious, but he had to ask. "Exactly how do you know that Chad wants to drive?"

"That's a good question, and it leads to the third thing that I think makes our team perform at such a high level week after week. We're '**doing life together**,'" Sam said. "If you think about what that really means, it's easy to explain how I know about his aspirations and goals: we talk." He grinned.

"Please tell us more," Sally said in a tone that expressed genuine interest. She recalled that she had heard that exact phrase, "doing life together," from Jo in one of their team meetings.

Sam said, "Let me ask you a question, Sally."

"Sure."

"I know you're married. Do you also have children or brothers or sisters?"

"Yes, all of the above," she replied.

"Do you know what's important to your children? Your brother or sister? Do you know their hopes and dreams?"

"I do."

"We know those things about one another here, too. It's more than a job. We are raising our kids together, taking care of our aging parents, sharing the joys and the tragedies of life together. We travel together. We play and we drink together. We win and lose together. When we win, it feels really good, and we share that. And when we lose, we feel the pain together.

"Here's an example. Matt is our driver. He crashed a few years ago."

Bob said, "I remember that. It was really bad, wasn't it?"

"It was terrible. We were at the hospital for four days—*all* of us. We're in this together. I'm guessing that when our time here is over, heck, we'll probably retire together."

"In a way, it sounds like you guys really love each other," Debbie observed.

"Well, actually, we do," Sam said unapologetically.

"Sam, this has been very helpful. We can see how **fit**, **practice**, and **doing life together** contribute to high levels of performance. Before we go, is there anything else you want to add?" Debbie asked.

"If you want to win in this business, it also helps to have a fast car!"

Enlightened Self-Interest

The first two visits had been remarkable. Debbie was extremely pleased and not really surprised that Sam and the general had very similar ideas about how to help teams excel.

As they prepared for their next visit, the team talked with the headquarters staff for the restaurant company and explained the objective of the meeting. It was suggested that the visit be with a local restaurant and not the headquarters. This was certainly *not* what Debbie had in mind. She was skeptical that her team could learn from a restaurant company to start with, and now, they would be meeting with the local staff, not the organization's leadership. This would be very interesting.

The good news in all this was that because it was local, Jo could participate in a field visit. The team asked Bob and Steve to join Debbie and Jo.

Before the visit, Bob sensed Debbie's reluctance and said, "Listen, this is perfect. If we're going to help our leaders take their teams to the next level, that's going to have to happen in hundreds of individual teams around the world. It's not going to happen at the home office. This is a great opportunity to get some insight into how teams might work in the real world."

Debbie wasn't totally convinced, but she promised herself that she would keep an open mind.

Jo contacted the local restaurant and found Amber, the woman who operated the business, very eager to help. However, she declined to meet with Debbie and her team alone.

"If you want the real answers, you need to meet with my leadership team. We meet every Tuesday morning. I'll check with them, but I think we can give you an hour on our agenda next Tuesday morning at 9:30. Would that work?"

Jo agreed and informed the others.

On the morning of the meeting, Debbie, Jo, and Bob arrived early to have breakfast before they would introduce themselves and ask to see Amber. Steve somehow managed to miss the car pool to the location, so he missed breakfast, too.

The restaurant was very clean, the food was fresh and hot, and the service was much better than they had expected. It was a great experience.

"If this is any indication of what we'll learn today, I'm pumped," said Jo.

Bob added, "Tom's research indicates that they are able to do this in locations all over the world—consistently."

"Let's find out how they do it," Debbie said, as the team approached an employee to introduce themselves.

They were greeted warmly by Tyler. They would later find that he was a new member of the team, yet he seemed completely informed about the group's visit.

"It's really nice to meet you. We're all excited that you'd want to visit with us. We're eager to see what we can learn from you."

Debbie said, "Thank you, Tyler. But we're here to learn from *you* today."

Tyler responded, "We'll see. I'm guessing we'll learn a lot from you, too. I'll find Amber—she's expecting you. Please have a seat."

The team was impressed with Tyler. He was very articulate for a young man who probably hadn't been shaving more than a year.

Less than two minutes later, Tyler reappeared accompanied by a woman in her late thirties. She was dressed in stylish business attire. Tyler said, "Amber, this is Debbie and her team."

Amber said, "Thanks, Tyler."

"My pleasure." And as he turned to head to the dining room, he said, "Thanks again for coming." Flashing a big smile, he was off.

Debbie's first comment to Amber was about Tyler. "He's an impressive young man."

"He sure is!" Amber knew Debbie was right about that.

"How old is he?" asked Jo.

"Sixteen."

"I knew he was young, but I was guessing eighteen."

"How do you get such high-caliber young people to join your team?" Bob was eager to learn what made Amber's team successful. In his heart, he knew already that people were going to be a big part of her story.

"Great question," Amber said. "But I only accepted this meeting on the condition that you meet with my leadership team. So if you don't mind, we'll hold that question until we meet them."

"Agreed."

"I'll be happy to drive," Amber offered.

"Drive?" Debbie was confused.

"Yes. We're headed to our meeting. It's already in progress, and we'll be joining them."

"Just a sec," Jo protested politely. "Already in progress? How can they do that without you there?"

"There you go again, trying to start the interview without the team. But I'll give you an answer to that one. That's part of the design. If they can't have a productive meeting without me physically present, I've not equipped or empowered them very well. And if our success is contingent on my physical presence, I'll become a prisoner of my business."

Debbie knew this was going to be *very* interesting. She was sorry that it looked as if Steve was going to miss it—he still hadn't arrived. She sent him a text with the address of the offsite meeting location. No response.

Amber drove them to a nearby bank building. She explained that the bank allowed them to use its conference room each week for the meeting. Amber said it was too distracting for her and the leaders to try to meet in the restaurant.

If our success is contingent on my physical presence, I'll become a prisoner of my business.

At 9:30, Amber and her guests entered the conference room. As she had indicated, the meeting was already in progress. There were five people on Amber's team. It was a diverse group—young, old, and in between. Four were dressed in a uniform of sorts, and one member was in a business suit.

"Welcome," said a young man in his early twenties. "We're finishing up on an issue. Please have a seat. This shouldn't take more than a minute or two."

The woman in the business suit said to the group, "So, here's what we agreed to. . . ." She reviewed several action items, including who would do what by when. The other four at the conference table nodded in agreement.

A young woman named Carol addressed Debbie and her friends. "So good to have you here with us today. We want this time to be valuable to you, and we'll turn it over to you in just a minute. But I thought we'd ask each member of our team to give you a sixty-second intro. And then, the floor is yours."

"Wonderful," Debbie said. "That'll be a great way to start." She was actually interested to hear the introductions for several reasons. One reason was to see who was in charge. First, she thought it was the young man who had greeted them; then, she realized it must be the woman in the suit who was summarizing action items. And then she got even more confused, because yet another "leader type" had set the stage for this conversation.

As the team went around the table and introduced themselves, Debbie noted their roles: there was an operations director, a marketing director, a hospitality director, a training director, and a quality director. The woman in the suit was the marketing director. She worked predominantly in the community—therefore, her different attire.

Each member of the team was very sharp and professional in his and her appearance and demeanor. Based on Debbie's preconceived notions, this didn't really look like a restaurant leadership team to her. It was even hard for her to grasp the idea in the first place. However, this was probably why this was one of the best-run businesses in America. She was eager to learn more.

"Now it's your turn," one of the leaders said to Debbie. "How can we serve you today?"

"We have lots of questions—questions about creating teams that generate outstanding performance over long periods of time."

"That's what we're trying to do. What's your first question?"

"How do you do it?" Bob asked.

"Well, it's kinda complicated," responded Kyle, the youngest in the group. He was probably only seventeen years old. "We do a lot of things."

"Just tell us some of them. We don't expect a formal answer with neat, clean steps. Just tell us what seems to work for you guys," Jo offered in an encouraging tone.

Debbie couldn't help but contrast this meeting with their meeting with the general. He had given his answer a lot of thought and had talked about three pillars. How would his answers compare with what they were about to hear?

"Okay," said Katrina, the marketing director. "What if each of us shares something we think contributes to our success as a leadership team? We'll see if that helps you and your team. I'll go first. **We treat each other like family**."

"Please tell us more about that." Bob's family was really dysfunctional. He wanted to hear about an "at-work family" that really worked.

With such simple prompting, Amber's entire leadership team began to share examples of how they created a family-type environment among the members of the team: celebrating birthdays, sharing struggles, helping one another at work and outside work.

Todd, the training director, added, "Some of us don't have the best family situations at home, and, of course, we can work at it and pray that this will get better for us. But for those of us in that situation, this family is even more important."

Bob realized that Debbie had always tried to create that same feeling in their team.

Amber, making her first comment, asked, "Who's next?"

Gwen, the operations director said, "**Good process**."

"That's an interesting response." Debbie looked at Gwen quizzically. "What does that mean to you?"

"Well," Gwen started, "I may need some help from the others on this. But as I think about why we function quite well and why we're able to get good results, it's in part because we have good processes."

Everyone on Debbie's team was taking careful notes.

"Guys," Gwen began, "what are some examples?"

The group quickly shared the following:

"We meet regularly."

"We capture action items and review them religiously."

"We're disciplined in our approach to problem solving."

"We hold one another accountable."

Debbie interrupted the discussion at that point. "I have a question about holding one another accountable. Isn't that Amber's role?"

Katrina replied, "Ultimately, but not in the day-to-day. We do that. If I don't do the action items I've agreed to, I don't expect Amber to ask me why—I expect this team to do that. If the problem persists, sure, it will end up on Amber's desk."

"That makes sense," Debbie responded. "Anything else?"

The ideas continued to flow.

"We do a review of our people every quarter."

"We review key data for the business at every meeting and develop plans to improve the results."

"Okay, time out." Bob was startled by the responses. "You guys are relatively young. How did you learn to do all the things you just outlined?"

Todd spoke for the team on this one. "Amber taught us. And, she encourages us individually to own our ongoing development."

Bob turned to Amber and asked, "What can you add to that?"

"Well, I knew that to build a multimillion-dollar restaurant organization, I needed people who could do all the things the team just described. I asked myself a simple question: Where are these people going to learn these skills? Are they going to get them at home? At school? At church or synagogue? I decided, if these things were important to our success as a business, I had to step up and provide them. I could *hope* that the team could do all these things, but hope is not a strategy."

"That's a real insight," Jo commented. "I'm afraid that in our business, we make a lot of assumptions about the skills people bring with them to the job. Do you remember what led you to this conclusion, Amber?"

"I remember it clearly. It was early in my career. We were struggling with our food cost gap—that's the difference between what we theoretically should be spending on food and what we were actually spending. A gap of a couple of percentage points on several million dollars is real money. I was frustrated. I had been talking about it for months with my team. I had challenged, encouraged, even threatened them, I'm afraid. We were still making no progress."

"What happened?" Jo could hear the tension in Amber's voice as she retold this significant story from her past.

"I was sharing my problem with my coach, and he asked me a very simple question: 'Does your leadership team know HOW to manage and lower food costs?' In that moment, I knew they did not. If they were going to learn it, I would have to teach them."

Bob interrupted Amber. "Did you say you have a coach?"

"Yes, I do. I've had an executive coach for many years. We talk on the phone at least twice a month. It's been extremely helpful."

"How has it helped you?" Jo asked. "Beyond asking good questions like the one you just mentioned," she smiled.

"In many ways—but let's stay with this example. I was struggling with the idea of teaching. It just didn't seem like it should be part of *my* role—I was the leader. My coach continued to challenge me on this. He gave me a book about Coach John Wooden. I'm not a basketball fan, but I am a fan of winning. And Coach Wooden was a winner. He was the legendary coach of the UCLA Bruins in the 1970s. He won ten NCAA national basketball championships in twelve years. I was fascinated that Wooden never described himself as a coach. Rather, he said he was a teacher and basketball was his subject. I've become very comfortable with the idea that a huge part of my role is that of a teacher. The restaurant business is my subject. And my leaders are my students."

"Do you teach others on the team as well?"

"Sure, on some issues—vision or strategy or things that they need to hear from me. However, I'm *not* the primary teacher for the entire staff. The men and women in this room serve in that capacity, along with our training staff."

Bob said, "Okay, here's what I've captured so far—along with a lot of great examples. Create a family-type environment, and make sure you have good processes. Anything else that makes this team work so well?"

"I'll add one," said Amber. "These guys might not say it, but we've got **great people** sitting around this table. We couldn't do 20 percent of what you've heard today if we didn't have the right people in here."

"You are an impressive group," Debbie affirmed.

"How did that happen?" Jo asked. "I'm guessing you didn't start with this caliber of talent."

"Well, we really did. You see," Amber continued, "we do have great people in leadership. But we also have great people in general."

"We know. We met Tyler." Bob smiled.

"The exciting news is that we have dozens of folks like Tyler. And many of them are candidates for this team in the future."

"Do you anticipate turnover here? Or maybe we shouldn't talk about that?" Jo made a face. Amber's entire team laughed.

"We talk about that all the time. Turnover is part of our business. Todd and Gwen are in college and will probably pursue a career outside the restaurant industry when they graduate. Katrina hopes to get her own restaurant to operate at some point in the future. And the others are undecided about their career goals. So, we're always recruiting, always training, always watching, and always talking about those to whom we can give additional responsibility. If this team is going to sustain its current level of performance, we always have to pay attention to our leadership pipeline." Amber said all of this in a matter-of-fact tone. It was clear that these ideas were embedded in the DNA of her business.

"This is really amazing," Bob added. "Not only do you do the day-to-day things extremely well, but you're also planning for the future in a very thoughtful and proactive way."

"Well, thanks, Bob," Amber said. "I will confess—it is a clear case of enlightened self-interest on my part. Some of these folks don't know what they want to do in the future, but I *do* know what I plan to do the next twenty-five years, and my success and my quality of life are forever linked with the success of this leadership team."

Debbie made a note: *If more of our leaders understood that simple idea, we'd be able to go to the next level with ease.*

"Any parting thoughts?" Jo asked.

Amber said, "I've got one more reason great people are so critical."

"And that is?" Debbie replied.

"We'll never accomplish our vision without amazing people."

"What is the vision?" Bob said what Debbie and Jo were thinking.

"To be the best restaurant company in the world." You could hear the pride in Todd's voice as he said it.

"That's huge!" Jo was surprised by the scope of the idea.

"Well, we considered being the best in the galaxy or perhaps the universe, but decided we'd need something to do next," Gwen said with a big smile.

"Thank you for your time today," Bob said. "You've given us some tremendous insights: **family**, **process**, and **people**, to name a few. It was very enlightening."

---

*My success and my quality of life
are forever linked with the success
of this leadership team.*

Todd said, "We're delighted you came to visit. It's a good reminder of some things we do instinctively." Looking at his watch, he continued, "Our time is almost up." He looked at the team and said, "We'd better get back to the restaurant. The lunch crowd will be coming soon. It's 'all hands on deck' for peak times. Thanks again for coming."

Amber had a request. "Can we be so bold as to ask you for a copy of your final report? We really do want to get better. We'd love to see what you find from your other visits."

"Certainly," Debbie said.

"When we get back to the restaurant, if you have the time, I'll treat you to lunch," Amber offered.

"Sounds great!" All this talk about the restaurant business had made Bob hungry.

On the short drive back to the restaurant, Jo asked Amber one more question. "Who is in charge of your leadership team?"

"Well," Amber said, "we rotate the facilitation role—six months for each person. That gives them enough time to learn the role and refine their skills. I found that rotating more quickly was not as productive."

"That's good to know. But I mean, who is the team leader?" Jo was looking for another answer.

"I think I know where you're going," Amber began. "I used to have a general manager—it was Brent. He's now operating his own restaurant. When he left, I decided to change my structure. I asked myself, What do I really expect from a general manager? Fundamentally, I wanted Brent to think about the *entire* business, not just a part of it. And I wanted him to care about the customers, the team members, and the business as much as I do."

"Sounds good to me," Debbie was listening from the backseat.

"It *was* good, but the more I thought about it, it was limiting. What I *really* wanted was *every* member of my leadership team to be a general manager—to think about the *entire* business and not just a part of it. I wanted all of them to care about the customers, the team members, and the business as much as I do."

"But today they said they have different roles: marketing, operations, et cetera." Bob was listening from the backseat also.

"That's correct, but if you think about the senior leadership team at your corporation, I'm guessing there is a marketing person, an operations person, and so forth, *and* they fulfill a general manager role as well. They think and care about the *whole business*, not just their area of expertise. We think about our leadership team the same way. Each of them has an area of primary accountability and subject-matter expertise, but they are all general managers."

Back at the restaurant, Debbie, Jo, and Bob enjoyed a hearty, tasty lunch. Steve never showed up.

"I wonder where he is," Jo said.

Bob frowned and said "probably sitting at his desk, reading the sports section or watching ESPN . . . and trying to figure out where everybody is."

The Big Idea

The team was eagerly anticipating its next meeting. Each member had ideas to share, based on his or her experiences "studying the best." When they assembled, they started, as was their custom, with a time of connecting and catching up.

Bob decided Steve deserved to be scolded a bit. "You would have enjoyed the restaurant visit, Steve. Lots of free food. And it was really good, too."

"Um . . . ," Steve began. "I overslept. When I got to the office, I saw you had already left. And I forgot where the meeting was. So I just stayed here and worked on some . . . um . . . stuff."

Debbie thought, *I really do need to talk to him about his attitude. But I don't want to do it in front of the team. I've got to make that a priority after this meeting.* She then quickly turned the conversation to Jo's mom. Jo would be leaving right after the meeting to be with her.

Debbie then transitioned the discussion to their visits. "Well, our field visits have certainly been interesting. Let's start by getting general observations from each of you."

This kicked off about forty minutes of great conversation. The team was excited about putting what they had learned into a format that would be easy to understand and hopefully easily embraced by their teams around the world.

"Let's look for themes." Debbie began to facilitate the debriefing session.

Jo began. "At the restaurant, I heard **family** and **good process**."

"Don't forget **people**," Bob added.

"Yes, and people."

"Okay. Anything else?" Debbie asked.

"A lot of good examples and illustrations, but that seems to capture the big ideas," Bob said.

Debbie quickly agreed. "NASCAR. Sally, what were your big takeaways?"

"Well, it's interesting. I'm already seeing a pattern. In my notes I have three buckets, and they seem to match Jo's list. I've got **fit, practice,** and **doing life together**."

"Don't forget the fast car," Bob added, and they both laughed as they told the others about Sam's parting words.

"Next, the general. He made it easy for us, because he had obviously shared his point of view before. Javier, will you tell us about the three pillars?"

"Sure. The general—or 'Roger,' to us—said building a team that consistently performs at a high level is a function of **selection, training,** and **esprit de corps**."

"So here's the summary," Debbie said as she turned to the whiteboard.

Big Ideas from . . .

The General: Selection, Training, Esprit de Corps

NASCAR: Fit, Practice, Doing Life Together

The Restaurant: Family, Good Process, People

The group looked at the board for a few moments, and then, all at once, they realized the pattern that Debbie had seen developing on the visits.

Javier spoke first. "It's amazing! They are all saying the same things!"

"You're absolutely right," Bob agreed. "They used different language, but the key ingredients for success in all these teams seem to be constant."

Debbie was eager to add her thoughts. "Before we reach any final conclusions, we have one more piece of data to consider."

"We do?" Javier asked. "From where?"

"Sally, do you have the envelope?" Debbie asked.

"I do." Sally pulled a small white envelope from the back of her notebook and handed it to Debbie.

"Before we started our visits, Jeff asked me to consider some internal best practices. He suggested that I reflect on the success we enjoyed as a team when I was in Operations and capture my key learnings from that experience. So I did."

"And?" Jo began with great anticipation. "How does all this match your experience?"

"Well, I put my thoughts in writing and sealed them in this envelope prior to our first visit." Debbie handed the envelope to Bob. He opened it and read what she had written.

> **To build a team that can generate great performance over the long haul, you must . . .**
>
> - Get the right people on the team.
> - Help them grow.
> - Create an environment in which genuine care and concern are the norm.

"I'm seeing a real pattern here," Bob said. "In all four examples, the same things consistently resurface." He went to the whiteboard and started moving things around and added Debbie's input. Here's what he ended up with:

Key Elements of a High-Performance Team

Selection, Fit, People, Get the Right People

Practice, Training, Good Process, Help People Grow

Life Together, Family, Esprit de Corps, Environment of Care & Concern

---

"How does that look as a summary?" Bob asked the team.

"Good. The patterns are striking to me," Jo said. "But I have a question. Are we calling these teams 'high-performance teams'?"

"We haven't really talked about what to call them," Debbie said.

"It makes sense to me. That's a good way to describe what we've been studying, and it is certainly what we want," Javier added.

"What do we mean when we use that term?" Bob asked. "How do you know if you are one?"

"It's more qualitative than quantitative," Javier offered.

"What does that mean?" Steve asked with a look of frustration.

"I'm not sure, exactly," Javier continued. "But I don't think we want to be very precise with our definition."

"What?" Steve was not satisfied with Javier's answer.

"Let me continue. We all want high performance. However, I think that needs to be defined in the context of the individual team. What represents high-performance for

Special Forces would be very different in NASCAR or a restaurant."

"It would be something different for each of our teams, too," Sally chimed in.

"Yes, but what is high performance?" Bob asked.

"When used to describe a team, it means that they have clearly demonstrated the ability to generate tremendous results for the organization," Jo remarked.

"It means they are not normal," Sally added.

"Are they abnormal?" Javier asked.

"Yes, but not in a bad way. A high-performance team has learned to apply the critical elements we discovered to generate outstanding results; and in doing so, they have been able to multiply the efforts of their leader," Sally explained. "They accomplish far more than a typical team—that's why we want to call them something different. They *are* different. 'High-performance' seems like a great description to me."

"I'm comfortable with that explanation," Javier said.

"If there are no objections, we'll call the teams we're trying to create high-performance teams," Debbie concluded. "Everybody?" She looked around the table and saw no objections. "Done. We're going to help our teams become high-performance teams."

"So how do we proceed?" Sally prompted, to keep the conversation moving.

"We need to think about a way to talk about the three big ideas that are integral to creating these high-performance teams," Tom said. "The key elements list is helpful, but what is the essence of each grouping? We need to simplify it some more."

Tom's question began a lengthy conversation about what each of the three elements really meant. Was there a way to capture the spirit and the intent of each? That's what the group was about to decide.

Jo said, "I've heard all the debate. I think the first one can be summarized as '**talent**.'"

Javier offered an alternative. "What about 'people'?"

Bob reacted quickly. "'Talent' feels like a higher bar to me. Everyone is 'people,' but not everyone is 'talent.'" The group laughed at the truth in that statement.

"So," Debbie said, "'talent' may be a good way to say it, but what do we mean by 'talent'?"

The team began to create its definition.

Talent is the first element in building a great team. It's a people-first approach. You need people who are a good fit. They need to have the desire and the capacity to learn and grow. They are people who enjoy being part of a team. Talent implies recruiting. Not accepting. Not settling. Talent is a higher bar. Great teams always have talented people.

Great teams always have talented people.

They all knew this description of talent would need refining but decided it was close enough to proceed.

Debbie said, "I like it! Let's try to do the same thing for the other two areas before we call it a day."

Steve groaned. *Will this meeting ever end? It's already a day. It's been a day all day*, he thought.

Despite Steve's eagerness to head home to watch the big game, the same process repeated itself for the second ingredient for building a great team.

"Okay, as I looked at all we've listed in this second area, it seemed straightforward to me; it looked like training was the key word until you get to 'good process.' Now training just doesn't seem to work," Javier admitted.

"Okay," Jo asked, "why would you think training?"

"Because people need skills," Javier said.

Bob said, "I like that, and I think we're close. Javier, think about what Gwen included in her explanation of 'good process.'" He referred to his notes. "She said it included things like

- They meet regularly and have productive meetings.
- They have a disciplined approach to problem solving.
- They do quarterly people reviews.
- They review business data.
- And they create improvement plans.

"And there were many more of these types of behaviors mentioned. The fact that they *learned* to do these things makes me very comfortable labeling them as skills. They were learned through training, but the outcome is skills, Javier. You're correct and you didn't even know it." He smiled at Javier. "The second element of high performance in a team is **skills**."

Javier nodded. "When you remind me of what Gwen meant by good process, it makes sense. I agree those outcomes sound like skills."

"Everyone?" Debbie was excited about both the process and the results thus far.

"Sally, are you okay with this?"

"Yes."

"Jo?"

"Yes."

"Steve?"

"Whatever," Steve muttered.

Debbie's concern with Steve was growing by the minute. She made a passing comment in Steve's direction. "We really do need your best thinking on this." No response from

Steve—just a look back at Debbie that said, "Are we done yet?"

"Tom, how about you?"

"It makes sense to me. Skills are what practice yields. It's what the general wanted as the outcome of his training, and it was what Gwen was actually referring to in her good process concept. As you work to help people grow, you want to give them skills. Skills seems perfect to me."

"Skills, it is, then." Debbie added it to the board.

"So, since we're all in agreement, let's write our definition for this one."

Here's how the team defined it:

Skills represent the critical element that separates wannabe teams from real teams. Skills represent a set of behaviors that can be learned and taught. It is the development and application of skills that enables sustainable progress and improvement. Without skills, a team cannot add significant value. As skills improve, results improve.

Skills represent the critical element that separates wannabe teams from real teams.

As Debbie thought about what the team had just discussed, she was reminded of some skill issues that needed to be resolved with her team.

"Okay, let's discuss the other item that surfaced in all of our visits. How can we clearly and succinctly represent this?" she asked.

As had happened previously, the team had a spirited debate. Periodically, the conversation would shift to trying to fully comprehend why this had surfaced in all three visits and in Debbie's past experience. As the conversation began to wander, Debbie asked, "Where are we on this?" There was no response from the group.

"Why is this so difficult?" Debbie continued probing.

"We're having a hard time finding a single word. As you heard, we came close on the idea of family."

"Why not family?" Debbie was pushing a little bit at this point.

Jo said, "You don't get to choose your family—but you do get to select your team. And for a team to be great, sometimes a change in the team is necessary. But if we call it family, and then we have to make a change in the team, that would be like disowning your mother."

"Not good," Bob said, frowning.

"Let's go back to the idea of choosing your family. Is this last element a choice? Really?" Debbie asked.

"Yes, it is," Sally said. "As we understand it, you can create the right environment, but you can't force it on people. You invite people to join; it's an individual choice. However, if we create the right environment, people will want to be a part of it."

"Let's take another look at something you said there, Sally. What are we inviting people to join?" Debbie was in full facilitation mode now.

"It's what we've got here," Tom said.

"What is that?" Debbie asked.

"It's like a community," Bob said.

"That's it!" said Jo. "We're talking about **community**. You can create it, you can nurture it, you can protect it, and you can invite people in. Yet it's a choice whether they want to join or not. And the best teams are the ones in which every member has willingly joined the community."

"So, how would you define it?" Debbie asked, and the team came up with this definition:

Community is a place where people *know* each other deeply, *serve* each other willingly, and genuinely *care* for one another. It is a place where people celebrate and mourn together. It is the element of a high-performing team that turbo-charges its performance. It is what makes the work more important than just work. It is the realization that you are not alone on the journey. It is knowing that someone always has your back.

Sally went to the board and wrote:

Key Ingredients for a High-Performance Team

Talent

Skills

Community

"I think this will work; it's simple and straightforward," Bob said. "I just want to be sure people don't miss the big idea."

Javier responded, "I thought this *was* the big idea."

"No, these are *elements* of the big idea."

"What is it, then?" Sally blurted out.

"*All three*," Bob answered emphatically. "If we fail to help our leaders understand the power of combining these three elements, their teams will never reach their full potential."

"Is it really important to have all three?" asked Javier.

"I think it's the most important thing we've learned," Tom said.

"Tell us why you'd say that," Debbie said.

"What we've discovered is not really three things—the secret of teams is the power of combining three things to create one," Tom said. "Think about what happens when a team is missing any one of the three. Without talent, the team is clearly limited. Without skills, talent will be wasted. And without community, the team never reaches that elite level of performance we've been trying to understand. Without all three, the team is doomed to be less than it could be."

What we've discovered is not really three things—the secret of teams is the power of combining three things to create one.

"Hold on. I hear what you're saying, but can't teams perform without community?" Javier asked.

"Sure," Jo said. "It happens all the time."

Everyone looked at Jo, shocked at her response. "You said *perform*," she continued, "Most teams do that every day. The question should be, do teams reach their *full potential* without community? Do they excel? Do they achieve crazy-good levels of performance? My answer to that question is *no*—not gonna happen. We heard it on all the visits—the general called it the 'secret sauce.'" Looking at her notes, Jo continued, "Sam and Amber talked about it, too. They said this idea was central to what made their teams so successful."

"If community is the difference maker, should it be our singular focus?" Sally asked.

"I don't think so," Debbie said. "If we already had appropriate emphasis on talent, and we already had amazing skills in every team across the organization, we might. However, I think there's huge value for us to focus on all three ingredients. As Tom said a few minutes ago, what we've discovered is not three things—it is one thing with three ingredients. It's the combination that creates the magic!"

"We'll need a word picture," Tom said.

"Does anybody have one?" Debbie asked.

"It's like making lemonade," Bob said with a grin.

"Really?" Javier said. "I've never made lemonade."

"It's simple—you need three ingredients: lemons, water, and sugar. If you leave any one of these out, you don't have lemonade."

Javier was clearly mulling over what had been said. "So, if our teams leave out talent, skills, or community . . . they'd end up with just water, sugar, or—"

"Just lemons!" Sally finished Javier's sentence.

After the team enjoyed a good laugh together, they agreed that one of the natural temptations their teams would face would be to focus on only one or two of the three ingredients. They decided to stress the absolute critical nature of talent, skills, *and* community; it takes all three elements to create a high-performance team. They all wanted lemonade!

Course Correction

The team's next meeting was intended to focus on how to begin introducing their findings to the entire organization. However, the meeting took a much more personal and productive turn.

Debbie opened the meeting as usual by asking everyone to give a status report regarding what was going on in their lives. They responded openly. After everyone else had spoken, the team members looked at Steve, who had always been reluctant to participate. After an awkward moment, he finally said, "All is good at my house."

"Anything else you'd like to share?" Debbie asked.

"Nope," Steve said.

"Okay, then, let's pick up where we left off in our last meeting. I still feel very good about talent, skills, and community. Did any of you have additional thoughts on this?" Debbie stepped up to the flip chart as she finished her question.

Steve said, "It's not very helpful."

"What's not helpful?" Debbie asked.

"That definition we created," Steve said in a matter-of-fact tone.

"Which definition?" Javier pushed.

"Community," Steve responded.

"I think it's a good definition," Javier said.

"Me, too," Steve agreed. "I didn't say it was bad—I said it wasn't helpful."

"Why not?" Sally protested. She didn't like Steve's tone.

"If I'm a team leader, you tell me that creating a high-performance team is as easy as talent, skills, and community. I know what talent means, and skill gaps can be identified and addressed, but I have no idea how to *create* community," Steve confessed.

"That's very interesting," Debbie observed. "You're right. In all three visits, our hosts stressed its importance, but we haven't talked at all about how to make it a reality in a team."

"Maybe we should give people a list of ideas?" Bob suggested.

"What kind of things would you recommend?" Sally asked.

"I don't know—share your life story, celebrate success, build strong relationships, give honest feedback . . . that kind of stuff."

Although those were good ideas, Debbie had a sense that there was another answer—a better answer. She tried to express her concern, although it was not fully formed in her own mind. "I don't want us to just give people a list."

"What do you want to give them?" Javier asked.

"I don't know exactly." Debbie confessed. "I'm fearful a list will become a checklist. And if it does, I'm not sure the result will be genuine community."

Sally said, "I guess we should explain it well enough that people can make their own lists."

The group just sat there thinking about Sally's comment.

"Maybe some principles?" Steve offered.

Everyone was pleasantly surprised, if not shocked. This was one of the few constructive comments they had ever heard from Steve.

The team began to brainstorm Principles for Creating Community:

Principles for Creating Community

Go slow—don't force it.

Celebrate the little things as well as the big wins.

Express gratitude and appreciation freely.

Find ways to serve others on the team.

Put the needs of the team ahead of your own.

Be vulnerable.

Think about activities you can do together inside and outside the office.

Make building community an ongoing priority—not an afterthought.

Never stop looking for ways to do life together.

Debbie looked at the flip chart and said, "I like it. These ideas should help our leaders build community at a deeper level. I particularly like the last one: 'Never stop looking for ways to do life together.' That's the essence of community. Thanks, Steve. Your challenge helped us.

"Any other issues that have come to mind since our last meeting?" Debbie continued to facilitate.

The room was silent. Everyone just sat there looking around the room. It was as if they all knew something, but no one wanted to say it.

Jo was the one who broke the silence. "I've been thinking a lot about these three things: talent, skills, and community."

"And what conclusions have you reached?" Debbie asked.

"We have issues."

"Yes, Jo. That's why we're launching this initiative," Debbie agreed.

"No," Jo continued, "I mean *we* have issues. This team has issues."

Debbie quickly looked around the table and saw more than one head nodding.

"Okay, Jo, what are the issues?" Debbie asked.

"Give me some help here," Jo said as she looked at the others around the table.

Javier joined in. "I think Jo's right. We *do* have issues."

Never stop looking for ways to do life together.

Bob said, "I think it's primarily a skill issue. We're generally good people, so I guess we're okay on the talent part. And thanks to Debbie's leadership, we've built some sense of community."

"Even before we knew what to call it," Sally suggested.

"I think you're right—our big problem is that we have a skill gap," Tom said.

"Is that it?" Debbie probed. Virtually everyone nodded.

"What would make you think we've got a skill gap?" Debbie was trying not to sound defensive at this point; she really did want to know what the team was thinking.

Bob said, "When we visited the restaurant team, they were looking at real data and solving real problems. We don't do much of that kind of stuff."

Jo added, "And Amber said that if she wasn't present at the meetings, they would continue in her absence. If you weren't here, Debbie, we'd all go home." She was trying to make a joke, but no one laughed. Her "joke" contained too much truth.

"So," Debbie asked, "what should we do?"

"We've got to figure this out," Sally said. "If we're trying to lead the entire organization to build high-performance teams, we'd better be able to do it ourselves."

Debbie had mixed emotions about this conversation. She accepted the team's conclusion—there were skill issues. She felt good that the team was comfortable discussing it together. However, she knew that ultimately this gap was an indictment of her leadership. And that hurt.

As a final dose of reality, she realized there was another huge problem that no one was willing to discuss. This reluctance was actually a strong indication of how far the team still had to go on their journey. Skill gap or not, there was a significant talent issue as well—Steve. However, Debbie decided to try to help the team work through the issues they had already uncovered. She knew in her heart that she was the one who would need to address the "Steve issue."

"What should we do about the skill gap?" Debbie continued.

That question launched a great debate. First, the group tried to identify the actual skills in question; then they engaged in an equally vigorous debate on what to do about them. Again, everyone but Steve seemed to be fully engaged.

About thirty minutes later, the team had identified the core skills they felt they needed to develop first—problem solving and conflict resolution were at the top of their list. And, perhaps most important, they created a plan to begin closing the gap.

Debbie was pleased with their effort. She said, "Talent, skills, and community. I'm thankful we've got a team that's willing to do the hard work to become a high-performance team. I apologize for letting us get off track."

In the short time that remained, the team decided to begin brainstorming ideas that would help them better train the organization on what they'd learned about high-performance teams. It was a brief yet productive conversation. Debbie was encouraged about the new trajectory the team seemed to be on. However, she knew she had a hard decision to make in the days ahead. She thought a meeting with Jeff might bring clarity on the issue.

. . .

It was a few days before Debbie and Jeff could arrange a face-to-face meeting. This delay was good. It allowed Debbie to think deeply about the issue as she saw it and decide what help she needed from Jeff. As was often the case, what she really needed was his perspective. Because he had been her mentor for almost two years before he became her boss, she felt safe seeking his counsel.

"Good morning," Debbie said as she entered Jeff's office.

"How's the project?"

"We've learned a lot about high performance in a team setting. By the way, Roger Grant said to tell you hello."

"I'm glad you got to visit with Roger. Was it helpful?"

"Extremely, and we've learned from others as well. But that's not why I'm here today. I'm scheduled to meet with you next week to give you a full report on the project. Today's meeting is about something else."

"What's up?" Jeff asked.

"I've got an issue with one of my team members."

"What kind of issue?"

"First, as you know, my team is not as strong as it needs to be, and I accept full responsibility."

"Debbie, you know how I feel about that. Every team can improve," Jeff offered.

"No, you don't understand. My team is not functioning at a very high level. In some ways, I'd even say we're actually dysfunctional," Debbie admitted.

"That's a very harsh diagnosis." Jeff still thought Debbie was being too hard on herself.

"It's tough in more ways than one," Debbie said. "I feel like I've failed my team and you. I am fully aware of our untapped potential and so is my team. They even challenged me recently on the skill gap we have as a team."

"That sounds like good team behavior," Jeff suggested.

"Yes, I guess it is."

"And," Jeff continued, "your team appears to have built strong relationships with one another. I think that's important."

"That's true too," Debbie said with a smile. "You'll hear more about that from us in our next meeting."

"So let me summarize what I've heard: you think your team is dysfunctional; the team pointed out to you that they feel they have skill gaps; you feel like a failure, and yet your team appears to do quality work and has built strong relationships along the way. Is that close?"

"Yes; however, you did leave out the part about our untapped potential," Debbie said with a faint smile.

"Debbie, what's the real problem? It sounds to me like your team is on the journey. I'm guessing you're just impatient because this team is not as strong as your last team."

"They were an all-star team," Debbie agreed. "But this team is different."

"How is it different?"

"With my last team, everyone fit. On this team, we've got a talent problem."

"What does that mean, exactly?" Jeff asked.

"We've been studying great teams—high-performance teams. They always seem to have the right people."

"And you don't?" Jeff asked.

"No, we have one guy who doesn't belong. Do you know Steve Hagert?"

"I've met him."

"He's never going to fit in," Debbie said.

"What makes you say that?"

"His attitude is unacceptable."

"Attitude is difficult to coach. What behaviors have you seen that would lead you to say he's got a bad attitude?"

"He's late to meetings. He's disruptive in some meetings. He doesn't contribute in others; when he does comment, it's almost always negative. Sometimes, he doesn't even show up at all. He checks his e-mail, or the football scores, or whatever during our meetings. He's rarely prepared. He doesn't offer to help other members of the team. And he's been unresponsive to my coaching."

"That does sound serious," Jeff admitted. "Why does he act like that?"

"Why?" Debbie responded. "Because he's disengaged."

Jeff corrected Debbie. "No, disengagement is the manifestation of something; it's a symptom, not a root cause. Did you select Steve?"

"No, I didn't. He came to our team as a result of the merger."

"What do you know about him?" Jeff asked.

"Not much, really. As I said, he's always reluctant to participate. He's the exception to your comment about 'strong relationships' on our team. He's not really part of our community."

"I see."

"What should I do?" Debbie asked.

"It sounds to me like you need to talk to Steve. Find out what's creating the dysfunctional behavior."

Debbie was afraid Jeff would suggest something like this. His recommendations were usually direct and practical. She had hoped for something less demanding, such as advice on how to create a severance package.

Disengagement is the manifestation of something; it's a symptom, not a root cause.

"I'll talk to him and let you know what happens."

...

The next morning, Debbie decided to meet with Steve— first thing. She knew this conversation was long overdue. She also knew that matters would not get any better if she continued to put it off.

She went to Steve's office. "Good morning. Do you have a few minutes to talk?" Debbie asked.

"I do," Steve responded in a tone that reflected his lack of energy and enthusiasm.

"Let's step into the conference room. I was reminded just yesterday that I really don't know your story. I know that you came over in the merger, and I know a little bit about your family but not much. Can you fill in the gaps for me?"

"Why?"

"Steve, I've noticed that ever since you've been here, you don't seem fully engaged in the team. To avoid reaching any false conclusions, I knew I needed to get to know you better. You know that I see my job here as primarily to help you and the other members of the team be successful. If I know you better, it increases the chances I can help you win—personally and professionally."

Steve had never had a manager tell him that the goal was to help him win. He'd had plenty of managers over the years who were clearly in it for themselves. This certainly sounded different. So, after hearing Debbie's explanation, Steve decided to tell her some of his story.

After about fifteen minutes of conversation, Debbie said, "Steve, this is hard for me to say, but I think I've failed you as your team leader."

"You have?" Steve hadn't expected that and wasn't sure what to say next.

"Yes, unfortunately, I have," Debbie said. "As I see it, we've only got two options."

"Only two?" Steve swallowed hard.

"One, either you don't need to be on our team," Debbie said in a matter-of-fact tone.

"Are you firing me?" Steve interrupted her.

"No, Steve, let me finish. Or, two, we've got to find a way to use your unique talents and contributions on the team. I think you'd agree, what we're doing now is not working. Listen to what I just heard in the last few minutes.

"You're an engineer by training, but we've put you on a client services team.

"You love solitude, yet your current workstation has four people in it.

"You do your best work when you can work alone, but we've made you part of a team.

"And, you prefer to start your days around noon. Our days start at eight! Steve, no wonder you're not engaged."

"Am I fired?"

"No, you already asked me that."

"So, what do we do next?" Steve wasn't totally sure what had just happened.

"Let's talk about it with the team."

"With the team?" Steve said in disbelief.

"Yes, maybe they can help us figure this out." Debbie stood and shook Steve's hand. "I'm glad we could finally get to the bottom of this."

"Me, too—I think," Steve said as Debbie left the conference room.

No Wasted Talents

Debbie walked into the meeting room the next day with apprehension obviously painted on her face.

"What's wrong, Debbie?" Javier asked. "You look as though you have a million things on your mind."

"It's that apparent, huh?"

"I'd say so."

"Let's start by creating a little community," Jo said.

"Great idea!" Debbie agreed.

Tom was the first to speak. "My new grandbaby said, 'Da Da.'" He was giddy—this was his first grandchild. He also had new pictures to share—he passed around his phone so everyone could take a look.

Then, as a huge surprise to everyone, Steve spoke next.

"Things haven't been good at home. This job is killing me, and I'm glad I've not been fired."

The team was stunned. No one knew what to say. Debbie decided to cut short the formal sharing time and jump in to try to help Steve.

"Steve, thanks for your transparency." Turning her comments to the team, Debbie continued. "I knew after our last meeting that in addition to a skills gap, we might also have a talent issue as well. Steve, I think we all know you are not happy in your new role. So, Steve and I had a conversation about his life, his experience, and his contribution to the team."

"What'd you decide?" Bob asked.

"We didn't. We—no, *I* decided to bring the issue to the team. Steve, thanks for bringing it up today. Steve and I

discussed that we would have to find a way for him to contribute on this team, or he'd have to work somewhere else."

"Really?" Sally said. "That feels harsh." She was struggling with having this conversation with the entire team.

"I'm sorry if it sounds that way. However, as your team
leader, I owe it to you as a team and as individuals to help
you win. If you're in the wrong job or the wrong company,
it's highly unlikely that you can win. I don't want you to get
to the end of your career and realize that you wasted your
talents.

"Did you guys know that Steve is an engineer?" Debbie
asked.

The team members shook their heads in disbelief.

Sally asked, "If you're an engineer, why were you
assigned to our team to start with?"

---

*I don't want you to get to the end
of your career and realize that
you wasted your talents.*

"Apparently, during the merger we didn't have an opening in Engineering," Steve said.

"And based on Steve's talents and experience, the organization didn't want to lose him," Debbie added.

"What are your talents?" Bob asked. The rest of the
team looked at Bob, surprised at the directness of his question. He knew what they were thinking.

He said defensively, "Listen, if we want to keep Steve on
the team, we've got to figure out how to use his skills. We
can't do that if we don't know what he's good at."

"Well," Steve began very slowly, "I am an engineer."

"What kind of engineering?"

"I had a double major in college—mechanical and industrial; and my master's degree is in statistics."

"Man! I never knew you even went to college," Javier said.

The group laughed out loud.

"No, no," Javier quickly added, "I didn't mean you weren't a smart guy. You just never told us anything about your past."

"Didn't seem relevant," Steve said.

"Wait a minute," Sally almost shouted. "I've got an idea!" Her excitement was evident. "Okay, our options are use your talents on this team or you go away. At our last meeting, we identified a huge skills gap. One of the skills we identified was problem solving and the use of, and analysis of, data. Are you people following me here?" Sally looked around the room. Based on the responses, she knew she needed to continue. "Okay, here's the big finish: Steve can be our subject-matter expert on understanding the data and lead as we try to solve the problems we identify. Heaven knows I can't do it, and I don't think any of you have the credentials that Steve has. What do you think?" Sally was beaming at her idea. And the others seemed to like it, too.

Javier looked at Steve and asked, "What do you think? Are you willing to give it a try?"

"I think so. I've always been interested in those things. Last week when I missed the restaurant visit, I stayed here and looked at the trends in orders from the clients we've lost. I found a few things that might prove useful."

"When were you going to tell us that?" Jo asked.

"I guess I would have shared it—if it came up," Steve said apologetically.

"Okay," Debbie jumped in. "Let's give this a try. Steve, we'll work to reduce your client load a bit—let's say 20 percent in the beginning. That should give you enough time to begin serving as our team analyst. Help us see stuff we're missing and understand what we do see. Are you willing to do that?"

"Yes, I am. Thanks for not firing me."

Everyone laughed again.

The tone and spirit on the team took a turn that day. Not only had they made a huge step on a major talent issue, but they had simultaneously made a huge leap toward closing a major skills gap.

"Let's take a break." Debbie could sense that a lot of emotional energy had just been expended. "We'll start back in fifteen minutes."

The Goal: Results

"Okay, what's next?" Jo was always interested in moving things along.

"We've done a great job deciphering what great teams do; now let's figure out how we help our teams become great," Debbie said. "Anyone have any thoughts on where we should begin?"

"Well, I guess we could share what we've learned with some people around the business and get their reaction," Javier said.

"Or," Sally added, "we could just start teaching our point of view on this . . . now that we've got one."

"What do you think the main challenge is going to be as we move forward?" Debbie asked the group.

There was silence in the room. It was a thought-provoking question.

"It may be budget," said Tom.

"Budget will certainly be an issue. But I'm not sure it's going to be the biggest challenge," Bob said.

"So, what will it be?" Debbie probed.

Bob added, "This is going to be a huge training effort."

"It sure is," Jo chimed in. "We have hundreds of teams around the world."

"Yes," Debbie said, "but we've done large-scale training campaigns before. I think we're going to have an even bigger hurdle to jump."

Steve sheepishly offered, "I think I know."

"What do you think?" Sally asked.

"Change," Steve said.

"Change?" Bob repeated.

"Yes," Steve continued. "This is probably a big-budget training effort, but it feels like an even bigger personal change initiative. The first thing that has to change is the leader. The leaders of almost all our teams are not focusing on talent, skills, and community."

Debbie said, "I think there's truth in all your answers. We have multiple challenges ahead of us."

The team began to talk about critical elements in a project of this magnitude. Debbie said she wanted to meet with Jeff and share the results of their work thus far. She added, "Thanks for your work on this! This has the potential to be huge for our business and our people. As we begin to focus more on talent, skills, and community, our leaders will grow, our people will grow, and we'll get better results. That sounds like a win-win-win to me. I look forward to our next meeting!"

The first thing that has to change is the leader.

Debbie was already on Jeff's calendar to share what they'd learned. She was excited to tell him what her team had discovered on their visits. As she prepared for the meeting, she was so grateful for Jeff's challenge and support over the years. She was a better leader because of his leadership—and she knew it.

· · ·

When the time came for her meeting, she showed up early. She'd prepared a one-page summary of the team's findings from their visits.

"Good morning!" Jeff said in his usual charismatic style. "How are you?"

Debbie replied, "I'm fine. Actually, I'm really jazzed. I think we've been able to summarize some important thoughts in a way that makes sense."

"Fantastic! What have you got?"

Together they walked through Debbie's document.

Helping Our Teams Move to the Next Level

What Is a Team? A team is typically a small group of people working together toward a common goal. Effective teams are characterized by trust and mutual accountability. Working together, they achieve more than they could working as individuals.

What Is a High-Performance Team? Our research focused on teams whose results far exceeded what would be expected from a typical team. In addition to phenomenal numeric success, these teams also enabled their leaders to increase their effectiveness and fostered significant growth among the individual team members. Our search was for the principles and practices that set these teams apart. We wanted to learn how they were able to consistently perform at these extraordinary levels. What did they do to become high-performance teams?

The Secret of High-Performance Teams Although we found different language during our visits, we found very similar practices among the teams that reach this higher level of performance. We believe that high-performance teams focus on **talent**, **skills**, and **community**. The key to their success is a relentless focus on *all* three of these key elements. A shortfall in any of these three arenas prevents the team from achieving its full potential.

Talent is the first element in building a great team. It's a people-first approach. We need people who are a good fit. They have to have the desire and the capacity to grow with the role. These are people who want to be on a winning team as opposed to just being individual contributors. Talent implies recruiting, and not just accepting or settling. Great teams always have very talented people.

Skills represent the critical element that separates struggling teams from successful teams. Skills represent a set of behaviors that can be taught and learned. Individual skills and team skills are both critical to long-term success. It is the deployment of skills that enables sustainable progress and improvement. Without skills, a team cannot add significant value. As skills improve, results improve.

Individual skills and team skills are both critical to long-term success.

Community is a place where people know each other deeply, serve each other willingly, and care for one another genuinely. It is a place where people celebrate and mourn together. It is the element of a high-performance team that turbo-charges their performance. This is the element that separates all great teams from those that are merely good. It is what gives additional meaning to the work beyond the value of the work itself.

The extent to which each of these three elements—**talent**, **skills**, and **community**—is fully present and developed ultimately determines the performance of the team.

Jeff asked a few questions along the way, but he seemed very pleased with the work of Debbie's team. "So tell me, Debbie, how did your visits match your personal experience of leading a great team?"

"It was kind of cool."

"In what way?"

"I did what you asked me to do. Before we started our visits, I wrote down my thoughts on how to create a great team and sealed them in an envelope. After our visits, I shared my notes with the team. My experience matched almost perfectly with the organizations we visited. It was one more confirmation for me that we are on the right track."

Jeff said, "I'm not surprised; truth is truth. The language can change, but the principles really don't. I like the way you've summarized your findings. What's next?"

"We're trying to figure that out. We know that this could require a substantial training effort and a budget to match." Debbie paused.

"And, what else?" Jeff asked.

"We think this is a really big change management project. Ultimately, we believe that a lot of our leaders will need to embrace a new paradigm."

"I think you're right. So how do you get that started?" Jeff wanted to know what Debbie was thinking.

"We're not sure."

"Okay . . . so what do you do when you're not sure?" Jeff saw a potential teaching moment in the making.

"First, I'd say we need to clarify the goal."

"And that is what?"

"Help our leaders take their teams to the next level, with the goal of creating high-performance teams throughout the company."

"I don't think that's the goal, Debbie," Jeff said rather matter-of-factly.

The look on Debbie's face was disbelief. She said, "You told us to 'study the best,' and we have. We've distilled all that we learned into an actionable, teachable point of view. We know what makes the world's best teams *great!* I'm confused." As she made that comment, Debbie realized she'd said that to Jeff before. In that moment, she was again thankful for his patience with her.

"Having high-performance teams is a strategy—a means to an end. It is *not* the goal." Jeff stopped as if he were waiting for Debbie to really think about what he'd just said. Before she could decide what to say next, he asked, "How are you going to visually represent your idea of talent, skills, and community?"

"We haven't talked about that yet," Debbie said.

High-performance teams is a strategy— a means to an end. It is not the goal.

"Here's an idea." Jeff went to the whiteboard. "We've got to be *sure* the entire organization understands that we don't want teams, high-performing or otherwise, for the sake of having teams. We *must* be sure that everyone understands that we're pursuing high-performance teams to enhance *results.*"

"Isn't that understood already?" Debbie asked.

"We can't assume that. Besides, why not help people get it just to be sure?" Jeff asked.

"I'm all for helping people 'get it,'" Debbie said. "What do you have in mind?"

"I'm not an artist, but I think a visual will help. You said that an effective team is always focused on common goals?"

"Yes . . . ."

"Is it safe to say, then, that a team that's not focused on performance improvement will struggle to be a high-performing team?"

"I agree—you don't drift to high performance, and you certainly don't get there without focusing on results." Debbie wasn't sure where Jeff was headed.

"So another way to say that is for a team to be successful, it must begin with a focus on results?"

"That sounds right to me."

"So," Jeff continued, "what if every time you talk about talent, skills, and community, you also talk about **results, too?** Maybe something like this. . . ." He turned to the board and drew the following:

"I like it," Debbie said. "It's simple—anyone can draw it. It shows that talent is foundational; it illustrates that you build *both* skills and community simultaneously; it also puts results as the focus."

"Results are the *real* objective," Jeff affirmed.

"Thanks for bringing that out. My team and I were assuming that calling these teams high-*performance* teams would be sufficient to communicate the emphasis on results."

"Let's not assume anything. The more we can remind people of the true goal, the better off we'll be. So, what's next in the process?" Jeff asked.

"I believe if we can convince our leaders that taking their team to the next level will help them improve results, they'll be eager to learn."

"So, how do you do that?"

"I'm guessing we need to show them that it works—in our business. Maybe we need to test the process through a pilot program."

"That sounds like a plan to me—or at least the beginning of a plan." Jeff smiled. "One more thing for now—what happened with Steve?"

"Thanks for asking. I appreciated your counsel on my last visit. I talked with him, and we determined that we weren't using his talents on the team. I found out he was an engineer, so we asked him to serve as our team's data analyst."

"And?" Jeff probed.

"And, we're going to give it a try. He seems excited. His engagement is definitely up since our last meeting. He also thanked me for my willingness to have a difficult conversation with him."

"I'm glad it worked out as it did. I know your greatest desire is to help people win," Jeff said, calling out one of Debbie's real strengths as a leader.

"You've been the one who has always encouraged me to do the right thing. That's meant a lot to me. Anything else we need to discuss today?"

"I don't think so. Please let me know how I can help going forward," Jeff said.

As Debbie was leaving Jeff's office, she had a flashback to all that he had taught her about leadership over the years. Today's meeting would be one more chapter in that ongoing story.

Launching a Movement

At the next team meeting, everyone was eager to hear about Debbie's meeting with Jeff.

"I had the meeting with Jeff that we discussed," Debbie began. "He was very encouraging. He likes where we netted out on the key elements. Talent + Skills + Community made a lot of sense to him. However, he challenged us to remember and to communicate: building a team is not the goal."

Bob interrupted, "Really?"

The entire group looked confused. To Debbie, this confirmed Jeff's concern.

"High-performance teams are *not* the goal," Debbie said. "The goal is *sustained performance over time*. High-performance teams are a *strategy* to get and sustain amazing results. **Results** are the real goal. It's a subtle but significant distinction. We have to ensure that the message is clear."

Bob added, "It makes sense to me. Results are at the heart of what makes a team high performing in the first place. High-performance teams are always focused on results—if they're not, you can be sure they're not a high-performance team."

"Okay, I can understand that distinction. It's a good reminder for all of us," Javier said, nodding his head in agreement. "What else did you and Jeff discuss?"

"We came to the conclusion that we should launch a pilot project. We can teach the concepts and allow our success with existing leaders to create the case for change to the rest of the organization."

Javier asked, "How will that create the case for change?"

Steve said, "By getting results."

"Not just results," Jo said. "Better results than they were getting before."

"What would be involved in a pilot?" Bob asked.

"We need to design and deliver training that will help our teams go to the next level. We need to teach them how to create high-performance teams," Debbie said.

"Let's do it," Javier said. Everyone nodded in agreement.

• • •

The next two weeks were intense as Debbie and her team interviewed leaders from around the country looking for teams to participate in the pilot. They also designed curriculum, arranged venues, and more.

One particularly interesting conversation came up around the possibility of creating a movement.

"I've been thinking a lot about this project since our last meeting," Bob said.

"Really?" Jo said. "I don't think of it as a 'project.'"

"What do you mean?'" Bob asked. "It has a goal, a budget, a plan, and a team assigned to deliver the goods. That sounds like a project to me."

"Yes. But projects end," Jo insisted.

"And this doesn't?" Bob asked.

Before Jo could answer, Javier said, "Not if we do it right."

Tom agreed. "The initial training and support will end, but if it gets traction—and it must if it's going to work—the focus on talent, skills, and community won't end."

Sally said, "Debbie, what do you think?"

"I think the launch may look like a project, but the ultimate goal is a movement."

"How do you define a movement?" Tom had never thought about this work as the launching of a movement.

Debbie went on to say, "To me, a movement is something that starts small, grows organically, grows in influence over time, and becomes unstoppable. If successful, the movement becomes the new norm, and the behaviors are sustained over time. If we're successful, high-performance teams will become 'business as usual' within our organization—part of our DNA. That's really what we want to accomplish."

The team ultimately identified twenty-five leaders who would be invited to participate. They divided the names and made the calls. The response exceeded their expectations.

The ultimate goal is a movement.

As Debbie and the team made their calls, one theme emerged above all others: all of the leaders, regardless of where they were on the journey to high performance with their teams, acknowledged the need to improve—and they all said they wanted help.

• • •

When the leaders assembled for the training, a general sense of excitement was in the air. The training was delivered over three days. The sessions were well designed, highly interactive, well facilitated, appropriately challenging, and provided ample ideas for implementation. The curriculum was built around talent, skills, and community. It was a big undertaking—that was clear. What wasn't clear: was it the beginning of a movement? Time would tell.

Harder Than It Looks

After three days of intensive training, the attendees felt ready to tackle the world. Debbie's team was elated. They could hardly wait for the pilot teams to report improved results.

At their next meeting, the agenda was focused on debriefing the event. However, during their opening community-building time, something amazing happened: Steve gave a report on what was happening in his life outside work.

"I told you a few meetings ago that things were not good at home," Steve began. "Since you guys were willing to help me expand my role on the team, I guess I've been easier to get along with. My wife had moved out. . . ." he stopped. The team seemed to be holding their breath wondering what he was about to say. "But, like I said, I guess I'm a little easier to get along with now, so yesterday, she moved back in. I've agreed to go with her to see a counselor. I just wanted to say thanks again for not firing me." He tried to smile but couldn't. "That would have been too much."

Debbie and the entire team were delighted that Steve seemed to be getting back on track at home. They also believed it was a really good sign that he would trust the team enough to share this type of information. A major contributor to genuine community is knowing one another and allowing others to know you. It felt great to know that Steve was willing to take this critical step as he moved closer to joining their community.

"Thank you, Steve," Debbie said. "Let us know how we can help." She paused, and then said, "Let's talk about the feedback we've received from the training."

During the next few minutes, the team identified numerous things they would do differently the next time around. But overall, they were very pleased.

"What should we do next?" Javier asked.

"Wait for performance to improve, the big bonus checks to arrive, and all of us to be added to the Executive Team for saving the company?" Steve said all of this with a big smile on his face.

"Sounds good to me!" Bob agreed wholeheartedly.

Debbie asked, "Until all that happens, what do we do?"

Tom said, "I think we should make some visits."

"That makes sense, but there were twenty-five teams represented. Should we try to visit all of them?"

"I'm not suggesting we visit all of them. What if we start by each of us going to see one of them?" Tom responded.

There seemed to be general agreement that this would be a good start.

"When do we make the visits?" Jo asked.

After a brief debate, the consensus was to wait sixty days. The team felt this would give the teams in the field ample time to begin implementing the ideas presented during the training. Everyone was assigned a team to visit except Jo and Steve. The team convinced Jo to stay home because of her mom's illness. They wanted Steve to begin the analysis of the pilot teams—look at their history, compose a control group of like teams, and create the evaluation criteria. The team wanted more than anecdotal evidence from their efforts. Was the training making a difference? Steve was charged with finding the answer.

Over the next two months, the team had infrequent contact with the participants. This made it difficult to really know how things were going. However, with the visits quickly approaching, the team was about to confront the magnitude of the challenge before them.

· · ·

Sally had been given the opportunity to visit a team that had been together for about five years. She arrived on site and was scheduled to meet with the team leader first and then the rest of the team. Roy, a twenty-year veteran of the company, was the team leader. His team was in the middle of the pack in terms of performance. During the training, Roy had expressed his desire to "make some changes" that would help his team grow and produce better results.

"Good morning, Sally. I've been looking forward to your visit," Roy said as he greeted her at the door.

"I'm glad to be here. Thanks for setting aside some time to talk to me about the team training and how it's working in the field," Sally began. "Before we get into our agenda, I'd like to know a little more about you and your team. And you may have questions for me as well."

For the next few minutes, they shared their history with the company and their lives before joining the company. Roy did, in fact, have a few questions for Sally, and she made a note of them.

"It's great to get to know you a little better. And I appreciate your questions. We'll get all of those answered before I leave today." Sally looked at her list of questions, and before she jumped in, she asked, "And what time will we be joining the team meeting today?"

"Oh, I'm sorry. The team is not going to meet today," Roy said.

"Really?" Sally tried to hide her disappointment.

"No. There's a lot going on, and we decided not to meet," Roy offered as his explanation.

team. One of the signs was the time allocated on the agenda to connect as a group. It reminded Javier of the way Debbie normally started their meetings. The balance of the meeting was focused primarily on improving the team's performance. Javier was pleased with the meeting. He knew that over time, this group was going to produce great results.

· · ·

At the same time Javier was visiting with Kelly, Bob was with Larry, a thirty-year veteran of the company. Bob had immediate concerns about Larry's team. In their opening conversation, Larry used the word "I" about fifty times! This fact alone made Bob both curious and fearful about how the meeting was going to go.

Bob asked Larry just before the meeting, "Who prepared the agenda?"

"I did," Larry said. Bob was not surprised.

"Great. One more question for now: who's going to facilitate today's meeting?"

"I will," Larry said, as they entered the conference room.

As it turned out, the meeting was a forum for Larry to tell everyone what to do. He not only told them what to do; he told them how to do it and when it was to be done.

After about forty minutes. Larry asked, "Any questions?"

There were none. Larry said, "Meeting adjourned." As everyone filed out of the room, a couple of the team members thanked Javier for coming, and that was it. Forty minutes and the only person who had spoken, other than a "Good morning" or "Yes, sir," was Larry. It was bizarre.

In total shock, Bob wasn't sure what to say after the meeting. Larry didn't have a team; he had a staff meeting. It was a classic "command and control" approach. Bob thought he might begin the conversation by trying to learn more about the team's results.

"Thanks for allowing me to sit in on your meeting," Bob said.

"What'd you think?" Larry wanted to know.

Bob was afraid he would ask that. "Before I answer that, how are your results?"

"Solid. We're at the top of the second quartile," Larry said without hesitation. Bob couldn't decide if Larry was proud of his performance or not. "Well, what does your team think about those results? Have you asked them how you might do better?"

"That's not really my approach," Larry said.

"Yes, I saw that in the meeting. The team didn't have an opportunity to contribute," Bob said.

Larry didn't have a team; he had a staff meeting.

"Well, I guess that's why I'm the team leader." Larry was getting a little defensive.

Bob knew he was on thin ice here, but he decided to push ahead. "Or, maybe your real opportunity as the team leader is to enable the team to be successful. I'm guessing they may have a lot of ideas on how to improve performance. One of the reasons we've embraced the idea of teams as an organization is that we fundamentally believe that together, we're smarter. We think that the collective IQ of every team is higher than the IQ of individual members—even the leader."

"I'm not sure I buy that," Larry said.

"You said you were at the top of the second quartile."

"Yes."

"How long have you been there?"

"For many years." He paused. "Decades, I guess," Larry admitted as he glanced away.

"Larry, you and I both know that your performance is not bad. Earlier, you called it solid. But solid is not stellar. My fear is that your knowledge and experience have gotten you to where you are, and unless you get a lot smarter, your performance and your team are stuck. You have become the lid on your team—and their performance. I'm not throwing rocks here, Larry. I just hope you'll consider what I'm suggesting."

"And that is?" Larry asked.

"That you begin to tap into the collective wisdom, ideas, and experience of your team. If you don't, I'm convinced you'll never get the results you really want. Please think about how I can help—I'm willing. But the first move has got to be yours." With that comment, Bob thought he'd said more than enough. "I hope to talk to you again soon."

"I admit you've given me a lot to think about today," Larry said as they shook hands.

• • •

Debbie's visit was to a team that had really struggled. She wanted to observe that type of team because she thought her experience from her time in Operations might be helpful.

She met Lynn, the team leader, for breakfast before the meeting.

Lynn began the conversation. "Thanks for coming to visit. I really can use your help."

Debbie asked, "In what way?"

"I understood most of the concepts you presented in the training. I'm just having trouble implementing them."

"What kind of trouble?"

"Let's start with talent. I don't think I've got the right people on my team," Lynn admitted.

"How many do you have total?" Debbie needed more specific information.

"Six."

"How many do you think are not a good fit?" Debbie was taking notes.

"At least two, maybe three."

"Okay. Let's talk about the individuals—their strengths and their weaknesses."

After Debbie listened intently for about thirty minutes, she said, "I'd love to help you more with this, but I'm afraid our time today is too limited. Maybe this is something you and I can discuss after the meeting today or perhaps in a follow-up visit?"

"That would be great."

"Are there any other big issues you're facing right now?" Debbie sensed there was more.

"One more thing for now is that my people don't have all the skills we discussed during the training. I think I missed something along the way. How are they supposed to get those skills?"

"You get to teach them."

"Me? I'm not a teacher," Lynn said.

"Teaching is part of your opportunity as a leader. Your people need the benefit of your knowledge and experience. They also need you to help them develop the skills to be successful. You can teach. You first have to decide that you *should* teach. The rest is preparation."

"And time," Lynn added. "I don't know if I've got time to teach."

"If you don't make teaching part of your job description, you'll never find the time," Debbie added. "And you don't have to do it all yourself, but you do have to ensure that your people have the skills they need to be successful."

"Yes. I've started making a list. I've already realized that there are two kinds of skills we are discussing here."

"Please tell me more." Debbie wasn't sure to what Lynn was referring.

"In the training, you talked about some of the team skills that our people would need—goal setting, problem solving, decision making, and even how to have a productive meeting."

"Yes . . . ," Debbie nodded.

"Those are what I'm calling **team skills**, and we don't have them yet. But the other types of skills are individual skills. I've been thinking about basketball. The skills you talked about are the equivalent of learning the plays. And

---

The real power will be unleashed when our team members have individual skills and team skills.

---

that's certainly important. But I have a new appreciation for the dribbling, shooting, and passing. Our people have to master the **individual skills** required in their jobs, too. The real power will be unleashed when our team members have individual skills and team skills. We need both."

"That's a big insight," Debbie said.

"Thanks, but it doesn't help me close the gap. That's what I'm struggling with."

"There's an old saying that seems perfect in this instance," Debbie said. "'A problem well defined is half-solved.' I think you're well on your way to a solution." She was encouraged by Lynn's level of thought and engagement.

"Let's go to the meeting," Debbie said.

"I'll introduce you and, at the end of the meeting, I'll ask you to say a few words to the team," Lynn said.

"I'd be happy to."

The meeting was relatively uneventful. Lynn's assessment regarding the skill gap showed up in a couple of places, but she stepped in nicely to keep the team on track. Her diagnosis appeared to be correct. If the team was going to be able to function without her physical presence, she would have to address a significant skill gap.

Her concerns regarding the talent on the team were less evident in the meeting. However, one of the members she was concerned about was not engaged in the meeting at all. Lynn had work to do, but Debbie was still optimistic.

The end of the meeting came, and Lynn asked Debbie to offer some thoughts.

"Thanks, Lynn!" Debbie began. "Thanks to all of you for what you're doing to take your game to the next level. We believe that together we can accomplish so much more than we can individually.

"I saw some great team behaviors today. I know that some of you expressed concern regarding your team's performance. That's a good thing. The best teams spend the vast majority of their time focused on improving performance. However, it was also encouraging to see you devoting some time to each other. You know we've chosen the term 'community' to represent the important dynamic of genuine concern for one another. It looks to me like you're well down the road on this. We believe this investment of time and emotional energy will pay huge dividends over time. If there is anything I can do to serve you going forward, please let me know."

Lynn asked the team, "Anything else?" There was nothing. "See you next meeting."

After the meeting, Lynn was very appreciative that Debbie took the time to visit. She said, "I've made a list of the things we discussed over breakfast, and I've added a few new things based on what happened in today's meeting. When can we get together to talk through these things?"

"I'm not sure, but I'll check my calendar when I get back to my office and give you a call. I'm thinking we can schedule a phone meeting next week, and I can come back for another visit in a few weeks."

"That would be great! I'd like to do what you did."

"What's that?"

"Go from 'worst to first.'" Lynn smiled. Debbie had never mentioned that part of her past. Obviously, Lynn had done her homework.

"I believe you can do it!" Debbie said with a huge smile.

$$\cdots$$

Tom was about to participate in a very interesting meeting. He had been unable to meet with Carl, the team leader, before the team meeting. So, he would meet him at the same time he met the team—or so he thought.

When Tom arrived at the meeting, Carl was not present, but everyone else was already there. So, Tom introduced himself to the group. They seemed glad he was there, but they had not been told he would be there. After about ten minutes of small talk, Tom realized the meeting had started . . . sort of.

Gloria, one of the team members, said, "Does anyone have anything to talk about today?"

Suzy did, "When is our department outing?"

Someone said, "I don't know. Didn't we talk about that the last time we met?"

Gloria replied, "Yes, we did. Nobody knew the answer to the question then either."

"Oh, okay. I just wanted to be sure I wasn't dreaming. I knew we'd talked about that before."

"Anything else?" Gloria asked.

Tom felt compelled to ask a question. "I've got a question, maybe two or three."

"Go ahead," Gloria said. "It's good to have a guest from corporate."

Tom said, "Are you the team leader?"

"Heavens, no! Carl's our leader."

"Are you the designated facilitator?"

"Nope, I'm just trying to keep the conversation moving."

"Two more questions: do you know if Carl's coming?"

Charley said, "Probably not. He went to some training a while back, and when he returned, he told us we needed to learn to operate without him here all the time."

"My last question: how's your performance?"

"Mine's good," Charley offered. And then each of the men and women present gave a very quick summary of their individual performance. They were all over the board on this, from terrible to leading the region. There was no mention or reference to the team's performance.

"Okay, I do have one more question. How can I serve you?"

"I think we're good," said Gloria.

"I've got an idea," Charley added. "If you see Carl, tell him we're doing good."

"See you all at the next meeting. Keep working hard!" These were Gloria's final words to the team as they adjourned.

Tom left the meeting with a sick feeling in his stomach. He knew that something in their training had been lost in translation.

Change Is Hard

Debbie checked in with each team member when they returned from their visits. She was glad the team had visited the field, but she was not excited about what they had found. Only one team really seemed to be on track. This was not the batting average they had hoped for.

The team was scheduled to meet on Thursday, and they would try to regroup and figure out what to do next. Much to Debbie's surprise, Jeff had called and asked her for a meeting. She wasn't worried, but she did wonder if Jeff had heard about the visits. Either way, she was glad to have the chance to debrief with him before the team meeting. She was sure he'd have some ideas on what to do next.

Wednesday morning at 8:00, Debbie walked into Jeff's office carrying doughnuts.

"Good morning, Jeff!"

"You remembered that I like chocolate-frosted dough-nuts. Thank you!"

"Just consider it a peace offering," Debbie smiled.

"A peace offering? What's that supposed to mean?" Jeff asked.

"Well, I figured you heard about our field visits."

"Yes, I did. That's why I asked you to stop by. I can't wait to hear the report."

"Oh, then you haven't heard. . . ."

"Heard what?"

"The visits were not good," Debbie said, embarrassed.

"Since I hadn't heard that, does that mean I have to give back the doughnuts?" Jeff smiled. "Tell me about the visits."

"As I said, they weren't good."

Jeff interrupted Debbie, "Before you go any further, tell me why you did the pilot."

"We did the pilot so we could make the systemwide introduction of our ideas more successful." Debbie hadn't actually tried to state the purpose of the visits in a single sentence before. She hoped it sounded okay when she said it out loud.

"Congratulations!" Jeff said.

"For what?" She wasn't sure Jeff had been listening. "I said the visits weren't good."

"Well, I do want to hear your report from the visits, but it sounds like, based on your objective, the pilot was wildly successful. Did it help you learn how to better introduce the ideas to the rest of the organization?"

"We clearly know some of the things that need more work," Debbie said.

"That's why I say congratulations."

Debbie was thankful that Jeff was a glass-half-full type of leader. She knew that his optimistic spirit was one of the reasons he was a great leader.

"Exactly what did we learn?" Jeff was curious.

"We're in the process of figuring that out. The team meets tomorrow to compare notes. I got a quick individual update from each team member when they returned from the field. However, the bottom line appears to be that only one of the five teams we visited is really on track. And, all the teams we visited seem to want and need some additional support."

"You said one of the teams was doing well," Jeff said.

"Yes. Javier saw a team that is doing really outstanding work."

"That's great. Obviously, that team only needed the information. Others will obviously need more."

"More of what?" Debbie asked.

"More help changing."

"What kind of help?" Debbie thought she'd ask even though she knew it was her job to figure that out.

Jeff went to his board and wrote:

$$\frac{\text{Motivation} + \text{Information} + \text{Assistance}}{\text{Change}}$$

"Virtually all training takes care of the Information part of the equation. And that's good. People need the information. However, change usually requires more than information. Some training goes beyond information and addresses the motivation of the learner, too. By the way, how'd you guys deal with the motivation issue in your training?"

"Inadequately, I'm afraid," Debbie said. "We were almost 100 percent information. We assumed motivation."

"Sometimes that works. But remember, change is hard. Motivation matters. And finally, the Assistance part of the equation is extremely important. Because . . . ."

Debbie finished his sentence: "Change is hard."

"You got it.

"Tell me more about assistance."

Jeff continued, "Assistance is all you do to make the change easier—not *easy*, but easier. Because change is hard, you must find ways to support the learning back in the real world."

"After the training event is long forgotten," Debbie added.

"Exactly. This can take on many forms: coaching, accountability, resources, communities of practice, and so on. It is the support after the event or, sadly, its absence, that renders most training efforts ineffective. Post-training support is where the real payoff lies. Even people who want to change and know how to change often need help to actually change.

"To summarize, it sounds like your challenge going forward is to do all you can to improve the information—but also to find ways to help with the motivation and certainly the assistance."

"We're on it," Debbie said as she jotted down Jeff's final thoughts.

The Real Issue

The next team meeting was scheduled for a full day. As the team arrived, Debbie could sense that the group was discouraged about what they had accomplished during the training. She tried to help them see that the pilot had given them the opportunity to learn and refine the training.

"I know you want to talk about the issues you discovered on your visits. That's the main purpose for today's meeting. But let's begin by identifying some of the good outcomes we've already experienced."

The group was slow to respond.

Jo said, "It appears that our message regarding the importance of talent, skills, and community got through to some of the teams we visited."

"The leaders were very appreciative of the training," Javier added.

"We have twenty-five teams consciously trying to get better," Debbie added.

"Four of the five visits generated excitement about continuing the journey." Steve was trying to find something good to say.

"Really, five of the five," Sally said. "Even Roy, whose team was not meeting, said he wanted to learn more."

"Thanks for sharing your thoughts. We've learned a lot about how to introduce an idea like this," Debbie said. "I didn't want us to miss those learnings. Now, let's shift gears and recap some of the big issues we discovered during our visits and see what we can learn that might help the next group we train."

This launched a very productive and eye-opening discussion regarding issues in the field. The team summarized them like this:

Issues from the Field
- Irregular/infrequent meetings
→ • Lack of role clarity (specifically the leader)
- Unclear on the big idea behind teams
- Command-and-control approach
- Leader readiness
- Team readiness
- Inadequate learning resources
- Lack of understanding regarding the up-front investment

As the team sat looking at the list, Sally was the first to comment. "Why?"

"That's a rather open-ended question," Javier suggested. "Would you like to say more?"

"Well," Sally began, "I wonder why we have those issues—what are we missing? What is the *real* issue here?"

Tom said, "There are eight issues listed, and I'm guessing there are eight different reasons."

"Or," Javier said, "maybe there are fewer than eight root causes."

Tom said, "I guess the training wasn't good enough."

"We can make the training better—and we will," Debbie said. "But I'm intrigued by Sally's question. Maybe training was part of the problem, but perhaps there is something else."

Javier said, "Let's go back and review the individual visits again. If we can identify and eliminate the root cause of the issues, we may have found a key to improving our overall implementation."

"Let's recap the visits at a high level. Who'd you visit, and what was their big issue or challenge?" Steve asked.

Each team member shared a summary of what they had observed in the field.

"Any patterns?" Javier asked.

"It looks like a leadership issue to me. That's the real issue here," Bob said.

"Everything looks like a leadership issue to you," Sally said.

"I'm serious," Bob shot back.

"Tell us more of what you're thinking." Debbie wanted to encourage both the critical thinking and the conversation.

"It sounds like Lynn and Kelly *get it* and the others don't. Almost all the issues in the field point back to the leader and his or her behavior," Bob said in a confident tone.

Jo asked, "What exactly is it the leader needs to get?"

"They've got to 'get' their new role in a high-performance-team structure," Bob said.

"Tell me again what their new role is?" Sally seemed slightly confused.

Debbie stepped in. "I think I can help. Let's use my leadership journey over the years as an example.

"Early in my career, I used what Roger would call the **command-and-control** approach. My 'team' wasn't really a team, but if you'd asked me to draw it back then, it would have looked something like this." Debbie went to the board and drew the following:

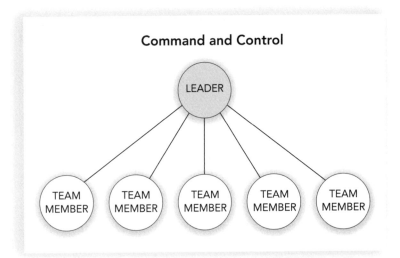

Command and Control

"That's the way Larry still leads his 'team' today," Bob said.

"Agreed, and we've talked about how challenging this is for the leader—and how limiting it is for the team. The work of our organization has become too complex and too demanding for a single leader to call all the shots.

"Later in my career, up until recently, I would probably have drawn our team like this:

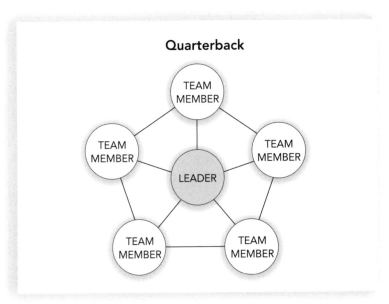

Quarterback

"We do collaborate more than in my early days, and you guys certainly add value, but an awful lot of decisions still come to me. I guess you could call this the **quarterback** model. When the ball is snapped, I'm probably going to touch it. Again, in a growing business, I don't think this is sustainable. I'm already at the point where I can't seem to get it all done. I'm slowing things down, and I'm fearful we're not tapping into the collective wisdom and experience of the team. That impedes results."

"So, what do you want the picture to look like?" Javier asked.

"I think a high-performance team needs to look like this," Debbie replied, drawing one more diagram:

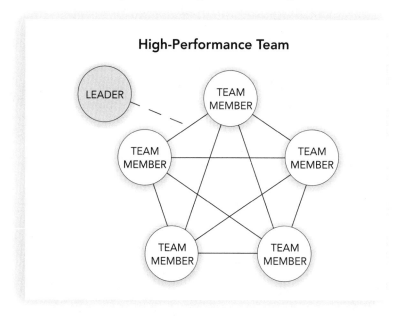

High-Performance Team

"In this picture, you guys manage your own work, and I have the capacity to actually lead."

There were a few nods around the room and a general sense of agreement.

"If we operated like that, it would change a few things for us," Javier observed.

"For starters, it would broaden your role and expand your responsibilities," Debbie said. That's one of the benefits of this approach—it would foster more growth for you and team members across the organization."

"So, I'm guessing you'd need to embrace a new role, too?" Sally said, unsure of how Debbie would respond.

"You are correct. I've already been thinking about that. I'll need to delegate more real responsibility, provide clear boundaries, teach more, and offer more encouragement along the way. This is the future as I see it.

"The way we make all this a reality is by continuing to focus on talent, skills, and community," Debbie concluded.

This was the first time she had shared some of these ideas with her team. Day by day, the future was coming into better focus. This new level of clarity was fueling Debbie's excitement about the potential of it all!

"Okay, that's helpful; but I'm still trying to ask a different question, a more pragmatic one," Jo said in a tone that bordered on exasperation. "After the leader embraces the idea that together we're actually smarter than we are when working individually, once the leader's committed to do the hard work to create a high-performance team, and after the leader understands that a command-and-control approach won't work, then what does a leader actually need to *do*? That's my question."

Everyone just sat there. Then Debbie said, "Let's follow that question and see where it leads us."

"So, what are the *specific things* a leader must do in talent, skills, and community? Let's try to keep the list short. This will require some discipline and prioritization, but I bet we can do it," Steve said. "Let's start with talent."

A few minutes later the team had created a lengthy list that was ultimately reduced to the following:

The Leader's Role: Talent

Identify the overarching talent needs of the team (current and future).

Always be on the lookout for talent—always recruiting.

Never compromise on character, competency, or chemistry.

The team believed that this level of clarity would be helpful for the leaders in their organization. So, they decided to repeat the exercise on skills and community. Here's what they concluded:

The Leader's Role: Skills

Work with the team to identify the skills needed for success.

Identify any skill gaps—individual or team.

Teach the team the skills they need.

Provide resources to help close skill gaps.

The Leader's Role: Community

Value community as much as talent and skills.

Be vulnerable and transparent.

Ensure the team invests appropriate time on community-building activities.

Always look for ways to help the team to do life together.

"This should help our leaders get started," Javier said.

"I think I was underestimating the role of the leader in building a high-performance team," Sally said.

Debbie added, "*Everything* rises and falls on leadership. High-performance teams are no exception."

A Second Chance

Debbie and her team knew they needed to refine the initial training they had provided for the pilot. There were some obvious things that needed to be changed, some things to be added, and even a few things that could be eliminated.

Based on what the team had found in their initial visits, they decided more visits would be helpful. Those would be conducted over the next thirty days. The team also wanted to hear from all the leaders they could not visit. They decided to send out a brief survey. Here's what they created:

- What impact did the training session you attended last quarter have on the performance of your team?

- What tangible success have you seen as a result of the training?

- How would you improve the training?

- What questions do you have that were not addressed in the training?

- How can we help you as you work to improve your team and its performance?

Five questions—that was it. The team sent these out by e-mail. The response was encouraging and almost immediate. With all this information—the initial visits, the additional visits, and the survey results—the team was ready to plan its next steps.

The team meeting was scheduled for Tuesday morning. However, Jo's mom died over the weekend, and Jo called Debbie to tell her that she wouldn't be at the meeting because the funeral was also planned for Tuesday. The team decided to move their meeting to Friday, so they could all attend the funeral service.

When Jo saw Debbie and her team at the service, she gave Debbie a big hug. "Thanks for coming today. You know you didn't have to," Jo said, trying to hold back her tears.

Javier said what everyone else was thinking. "We know we didn't *have* to. We wanted to be here to show you we care."

It's comforting to know that you really don't have to do life alone.

"I appreciate that so much!" This time Jo hugged Javier. "I've got to be with my family. Thank you so much for coming. I'll see you back in the office." As she walked away, she looked over her shoulder and gave the group a look full of gratitude.

Bob turned to the group and said, "In case we ever forget what community really means, we should remember this moment."

"It's comforting to know that you really don't have to do life alone—to know that you've got somebody who'll be there in the good times and the bad. That's really wonderful," Sally said.

There was silent agreement among the team. They could feel the power of community.

. . .

Friday morning, the meeting began with Jo thanking everyone for attending the funeral. "It was great to have you all there."

There were several other updates, and then the focus shifted to the next item on the agenda. It simply read, "High-Performance Teams—Next Steps?"

Debbie asked Javier to lead the discussion. Ever since the team acknowledged the skills that were underdeveloped, she had been teaching more and actually doing less to facilitate the team meetings. It was a small step, but much needed. She was still struggling with personal capacity issues, but something as simple and tangible as someone else facilitating the meeting gave her reason to hope that she could ultimately take back her schedule—and her life.

Javier began by framing the topic. "We've gotten a lot of tremendous feedback on last quarter's training session. The visits have been very enlightening, and the survey results have helped as well. Now we have to decide what to do next."

"What is the organizational expectation?" Bob asked.

"What does Jeff expect?" Sally added.

"One question at a time, please," Javier said. "Let's start with Bob's question. The organizational expectation is that we help our teams go to the next level, because we believe that will increase our performance. The great news is that we're confident we've found the answer."

"Leaders who are willing to do the hard work—the ones willing to focus on talent, skills, and community—can create high-performance teams," Tom said.

"You got it," Javier said.

"So, the question is, how do we get the message out?" Jo said.

"That's partially it. Unfortunately, I'm afraid it's more challenging than that," Tom said. "'Getting the message out' sounds like a communications effort. You could say that's what we did in the first session of the pilot with the leaders. We gave them a lot of information.

"I'm going back to something we discussed some time ago—this is really a change management issue.

Communication is part of it, but we're going to have to do a lot more than share information."

"I think our visits confirmed that," Sally added.

Debbie reflected on what Jeff had said about helping people change. "How can we strengthen the motivational aspect of the program?"

The team brainstormed dozens of great ideas. One they really liked was to have an opening address by Jeff at future meetings.

"That brings up a good question," Bob said. "Are we focused solely on the next training session, or are we going to do anything else with the pilot group?"

After some debate, the team decided to reconvene the pilot leaders. They decided that if they could help these teams be successful, their stories would really help with the motivation factor for the balance of the leaders across the organization. The team also realized that unless they invested more time with the pilot group, results and positive testimonies would be unlikely.

So they began creating two lists: what they would do with the pilot leaders on their second visit, and what they would want to do during the new and improved training session for the rest of the organization. In an ideal world, perhaps these would be separate phases of the project, but the urgency of the situation would dictate developing con-current plans of attack.

With several good ideas on how to increase the motiva-tion element of their change effort, Debbie shifted the con-versation to how they could offer more assistance with the change. "What can we do to help our leaders after the initial training?"

Again, this question sparked a great discussion leading to many good ideas. Jo recorded the following items: more follow-up consulting visits, training resources, webinars, phone coaching, recurring training, user groups, best practice visits, and ongoing communication.

"Ongoing senior leadership support will be extremely important," Bob said. "It's great that Jeff and the Executive Team are supportive of this." He paused. "I've been here a long time. I've seen a lot of very important things—strategies and plans—come and go. This one seems bigger and more difficult than anything we've ever attempted. That's why I think our chances for success are really slim if we can't continue to keep Jeff and other senior leaders focused on this."

Ongoing senior leadership support will be extremely important.

"Thanks, Bob. That really does need to be on the list," Debbie said, affirming his response and his candor. "This is a big deal. What we're attempting is very difficult, and you're right—people throughout the organization are going to be looking for cues from leadership regarding their level of support."

"That's an outstanding list. Thanks, Jo, for helping us with that," Javier said. "Now let's talk about what we'll do with our pilot leaders at their second session."

"And let's decide what kind of post-training support we can provide for them," Sally suggested. "It would have been better to do it after the first session, but to me, it doesn't seem to be too late."

The team began to create the plan for the next stage of the journey.

The Journey Continues

The team developed two comprehensive plans: one for the pilot leaders and another for a systemwide introduction of the high-performance team concepts.

Debbie met with Jeff and reviewed the plans. He liked them both. He also decided to speak to the pilot team leaders when they returned for their second session. He wanted them to hear directly from him how important this work was to the long-term health and vitality of the organization.

He also agreed to talk to as many of the other groups as possible when the systemwide launch began. When he couldn't be present, he volunteered members of the Executive Team to be there. He understood that ongoing leadership support would be vital.

The team reconvened the original pilot leaders and opened with a session in which the attendees were invited to share their questions and issues regarding the project.

This was followed with a session entitled "Lessons Learned from the Field," presented by Debbie's team. The short list of critical roles the leader must play in talent, skills, and community was extremely well received.

The final session included a brief message from Jeff. His comments about the journey were inspiring.

"Today, I am privileged and honored to stand before the most remarkable group of men and women with whom I have ever worked. Your spirit of optimism and your confidence inspire me. I know that you care about the future—not just your personal future but the future of your teammates and of our company. I know that you care about our customers and about providing the quality products and services they expect and deserve. I know that you care about outshining the competition in every detail.

"That's why it's so heartening to me that you were all willing and eager to become involved in a pilot program designed to help all your teams and our company go to the next level.

"The challenges we face are real and urgent. We have more competition than we've had in the past, and the complexity of our business continues to increase. On top of that, our customers are more demanding and have higher expectations than ever. Because of all these factors, you and leaders across the organization are working harder than ever just trying to keep up with it all. That's one of the major reasons we're excited about helping you build high-performance teams. We can see a day when your team will multiply your leadership effort and your impact many times over.

"Just a few short months ago, I asked Debbie Brewster and her team to help us find the secret of teams. They found it, and you are validating it. When you select **talent** for your teams, make sure to help your team members build the necessary **skills**, and create a strong **community**, you can achieve results we previously thought impossible. However, it all begins with your **leadership**. With your leadership, we can move into the future with new levels of confidence and new levels of performance—performance that will be the envy of our industry. We need you, and your teams, to rise to the occasion and take command of our future. To all of you—and to everyone on your teams—*thank you!*"

Jeff followed these brief remarks with a town hall-style question-and-answer session. The leaders loved this approach. Jeff helped set the right tone—an appropriate blend of urgency and optimism.

The pilot group left with a fresh sense of energy and focus. Armed with many of the answers they had been looking for, they were poised for real progress. They also had a new level of confidence that they could help their teams become high-performance teams. Debbie and her team knew that combining this new optimism with the post-training support should be a recipe for amazing results.

The plan was to work with the pilot leaders in the field for several months. Along the way, Debbie and her team would be looking for success stories. These stories from the field would be featured in the systemwide introduction of the high-performance team concepts.

• • •

A few weeks later, Debbie asked the team to come to the next meeting ready to share what they were seeing in the field.

The meeting began as usual with a time to strengthen community. Tom had new pictures of his grandbaby. Javier had received a letter from his mom, and Jo had just settled her mom's estate. Debbie announced that she was training for her first triathlon. The group was impressed.

Sally asked, "Does that have anything to do with guns?"

"No," Tom said. "I think you've got it confused with a pentathlon. That event involves shooting."

"Yes, thank goodness—no guns. Just running, biking, and swimming," Debbie said.

"Please keep us posted on your progress," Javier said.

Steve took the opportunity to thank the entire team for their support. "As I look back on the last few months, I know I was difficult, even rude, in some of our meetings. I knew I wasn't using my gifts; things weren't good at home. I was frustrated. Thanks for not giving up on me."

Debbie was next to speak. "Thanks to all of you for your hard work over the last few months. We've done a lot of work—outstanding work—quickly. I'm confident we're going to see results from our efforts, and we may even see the first of those results today as we hear reports from the field. I've asked Jo to be our facilitator today. Jo, take it away."

"Thanks, Debbie, for allowing me to facilitate today. This is one of those skills I need to sharpen a bit. I look forward to getting feedback from each of you at the end of the meeting. As Debbie said, our topic today: what are we seeing in the field? Who wants to start?"

"I have an amazing, 'believe-it-or-not' report," Sally said. The team could tell she was really excited.

"Well, tell us!" Jo said in a tone that matched Sally's.

"I went back to the team I visited a few months ago."

"The one that wasn't meeting?" Javier asked.

"Yes, that one. You won't believe it. Not only are they meeting, but it's working!" Sally said.

"What do you mean by 'working'?" Tom asked.

"They're doing exactly what we taught in the training, and it's bringing purpose and direction to the team," Sally began. "The best part is that Roy, the leader, has seen the light. Remember his concern that having meetings caused lost productivity? I challenged him to run an 'experiment' and meet with his team for a ninety-minute, focused meeting every week for eight weeks. If he didn't think he could see any benefits, he could reevaluate. He took it seriously, and the team brought so many improvement ideas to the table, Roy became a believer. They're a great success story!"

"Did anyone else go back to a team they'd visited previously?" Jo asked.

"Yes, I did," Bob said. "Larry is still a command-and-control guy at heart. He's not going to change. However, he has begun to involve his team more. His team is still skeptical, but their results have improved some. I wouldn't call it a success story yet. Their ultimate success is in Larry's hands.

I'm encouraged by the early results. But having the right talent starts with having the right leader, and Larry may not be the right leader. Time will tell."

Debbie spoke next. "I went back to see Lynn. Her team is making great progress. They started by doing some really hard work."

Jo said, "Remind us—what was their big issue?"

"They had two: talent and skills. I guess you could say they had three, because the talent and skills issues were certainly impeding community.

Having the right talent starts with having the right leader.

"But as I said, they're making real progress. Lynn had to terminate one team member and transfer another. They just weren't a good fit. One was a raw talent issue, and the one who was terminated just didn't want to be part of a team.

"Regarding skills, Lynn has been very deliberate to identify the key skills the team needs, and she's been systematically teaching them."

"Where'd she start?" Javier said.

"You may not believe this," Debbie said, "but she started with 'Business 101.' She revisited the basic economics of our business—how we make money and a complete review of the profit-and-loss statement. She challenged her team not to review the monthly reports in order to see what *had* happened, but instead to plan their activities in advance to impact what was *going* to happen. She told them the reports were merely a reflection of what the team had done or had failed to do."

"What a wonderful way to frame their role!" Tom said. "That is powerful. I think we'll definitely want her to speak at the next training session."

"Give her time," Debbie said, encouraging some restraint. "Remember, Lynn's team was the worst in the organization, and she has two new team members. It's early."

"What does your gut tell you?" Javier asked.

"She's going to be a rock star!" Debbie was beaming.

"What else are we seeing out there?" Jo asked the group. The team listed the following:

Good Signs of Progress in the Field

Most of the pilot teams are experiencing better results.

Cost and productivity concerns have been largely offset by the results.

Individual team member engagement appears to be improving.

Numerous volunteers are helping us "tell the story" to others.

Leaders are asking for additional learning resources.

There's better understanding of the journey and the time commitment required.

This process has accelerated the development of our next generation of leaders.

Even teams that hadn't been meeting were having productive meetings.

"It's early, but these are incredibly positive signs. I think we're ready to challenge and equip the rest of the organization," Jo said in summary.

The balance of the meeting was focused on how to incorporate all they had learned thus far into the systemwide introduction. The plan was finalized. The team was ready. Every member was excited about the possibilities.

At the end of the meeting, Debbie knew the organization was about to take a giant leap forward. She was grateful that her team was taking the necessary steps to make it to the next level as well. They weren't a high-performance team yet, but she was optimistic. She wanted to say something, but she had nothing prepared. So she decided to say what was in her heart: "I'm grateful to be on this journey with each of you!"

Conclusion:
The Next Step Is Yours

How do you write an ending to a story that never ends? That's the challenge I face at this moment. Creating high-performance teams may start as a project; it may even be described as a strategy—and it's certainly a powerful one. Perhaps it will become a movement, as Debbie envisioned. If you stick with it, it can certainly create competitive advantage. Or who knows? Over time, it could even become part of your organization's DNA.

However, pursuing high-performance teams can be so much more than that. It can not only turbo-charge your performance as a team but also significantly multiply your impact as a leader! It may be the ultimate win-win-win-win that most organizations are seeking: customers win, employees win, leaders win, and shareholders win.

So what's next for you? I have five specific actions for you to consider:

1. Evaluate your current reality. Reality is a leader's best friend. What are the facts? How well is your team currently performing? Do you even have a team? What are the trends? What will the future hold? What do you want to be true in the future? Will your current approach get you where you want to go? How is your quality of life? I'm suggesting a full environmental scan. Armed with the facts, you're ready for step 2. . . .

2. Assess your team's talent. Talent is foundational. Do you have the right players to help you build a high-performance team? What does each member bring to the table? Are they committed to lifelong learning? Do they want to be part of something bigger than themselves? Are they team players? Do you have adequate functional diversity? (There's a simple assessment in the back of this book to help you get started.)

3. Assess your team's skills. Take a hard look at both the individual and the team skills within your group. What are the critical skills needed for your team to excel? What is your plan to close any skill gaps that you discover? Don't try to attack them all at once. Prioritize. Get the team to help. Don't miss the opportunity to teach, and don't assume you have to do it all alone. Find resources to help close the gaps.

4. Build genuine community. Start today, regardless of where you are on the journey. It will take time—don't waste a day. Building community is a process that requires ongoing attention from you and the team. How can you create opportunities for the team members to better know each other? Serve each other? Celebrate each other's victories—large and small? How can you help the team do life together? Take it on faith if you can receive it no other way: building community will be worth every minute you invest. If done well, it will also provide tremendous joy and satisfaction along the way.

5. Lead at the next level. Creating high-performance teams will require no less leadership than you're providing today; however, it may require a different kind of leadership: invest in talent, skills, and community; cast vision; delegate real responsibility—not just tasks; teach; encourage; set boundaries; provide resources; and set the expectation that the team will manage their own work. Neither Debbie's team nor her organization drifted to high performance. Your organization will not drift there either. The journey to becoming a high-performance team always begins with leadership. That's what Debbie and Jeff provided. That's your challenge and mine.

Let me encourage you to stay the course—and enjoy the journey!

High-Performance Team Assessment

Rate each statement using the following scale:

5 = Completely Agree; **4** = Partially Agree; **3** = Neither Agree nor Disagree; **2** = Partially Disagree; **1** = Completely Disagree

Talent	**Your Rating**
Every member of the team thinks holistically about the business.	___
Every member of the team is a team player.	___
The team members represent diverse perspectives on the business.	___
The team members are committed to personal and professional growth.	___
The individual members of the team are in the right roles within the organization.	___
Talent Total:	___

Skills

The team has a disciplined approach to problem solving that works.	___
Data plays a critical role in the team's efforts to solve problems.	___
The team is capable of conducting an effective meeting.	___
The team has demonstrated the ability to resolve conflict within the team.	___
Individual members of the team possess the skills needed to do their job well.	___
Skills Total:	___

Community

The team members know each other's story
(personal and professional).   ___

The team members care deeply about every other
member of the team.   ___

The team regularly celebrates the accomplishments
of individual members.   ___

Members of the team go out of their way to serve
each other.   ___

The team is doing life together.   ___

Community Total: ___

Leadership

The leader communicates a clear vision for the
future of the team.   ___

The leader delegates real responsibility to the team.   ___

The leader expects the team to manage their own work.   ___

The leader has established clear boundaries for the team.   ___

The leader encourages the team and the individual
members.   ___

Leadership Total: ___

Next Steps

After you've completed this assessment, consider asking your team
to do the same. Compare your answers. Talk about the statements
where your ratings are significantly different. Involve the team
in creating a plan for improvement. Repeat the assessment in six
months. Celebrate your progress!

Acknowledgments

There are so many people to thank for their contributions to this project; in every sense, it has been a team effort. I'll just start at the beginning.

More than twenty years ago, Dan Cathy challenged our organization to learn all that we could about teams. Thanks to Dan for his insight and visionary leadership—he was right about the power of teams.

In my search for mentors on the topic of teams, I found many. But two far surpass all others: Jennifer Howard and Larry Miller. They introduced me to the skills and the discipline required to make teams a reality.

It was also over twenty years ago that we quickly discovered that there was something that separated the good teams from the great ones. Jon Katzenbach helped give language to what we were feeling and experiencing. His groundbreaking work, *The Wisdom of Teams*, was extremely helpful.

Bill Hybels, the senior pastor of Willow Creek Community Church in Chicago, helped us give voice to the idea of community. Some of his ideas are found on the pages of this book. Bill also gave us the language around character, competence, and chemistry. Thanks, Bill, for continuing to help me grow in my leadership.

Closer to home, I must thank the Training and Development team at Chick-fil-A. They challenge my thinking. They make our organization better. I love the team we've built together over the last decade. Specifically, I want to acknowledge the work of Mark Conklin, Cathy Price, Beth

Pelfrey, and Michelle Oates. They are the core team that is bringing this material to life within our organization. They have become the subject-matter experts on what you've just read. They have not only shaped this content; they've made it much better than it would have been otherwise.

Bill Dunphy, Andy Lorenzen, and Justin Whitfield, thanks for your feedback during the process. Thanks to Tim Tassopoulos for asking me to write this book and providing outstanding feedback on the early manuscript.

Special thanks go to Chick-fil-A Operators everywhere. Over the past thirty years, I've watched them build teams in their restaurants. Many of the ideas shared in *The Secret of Teams* have their origins in the practices of these outstanding business leaders.

Steve Gottry, Steve Piersanti, Janice Rutledge, and Laura Larson served as amazing editors and thinking partners. Each of them made significant contributions to this effort. Thank you!

My wife, Donna, has read this manuscript several times. Her candor is refreshing and extremely helpful. If you ever meet her, you should thank her.

Teneya Fouts played a *huge* role in the success of this project, as she does in all the work that I do. She keeps me headed in the right direction and brings me back when I do stray off course. Thank you!

John Dodson, the community/NASCAR team relations director at NASCAR Technical Institute, thank you for helping us learn more about racing.

Savannah Wallace, thank you for helping with the graphics.

And, to all of you who will join us on the journey to create high-performance teams, thanks for investing your time to read *The Secret of Teams*!